REAL
-PEOPLE-
REAL FAITH

REAL -PEOPLE- REAL FAITH

KESWICK MINISTRY

Donald English on 1 Corinthians
Stuart Briscoe on James
PLUS many other Messages

Edited by David Porter

STL Books

PO Box 48, Bromley, Kent, England.
PO Box 28, Waynesboro, Georgia, USA.
PO Box 656, Bombay 1, India.

Keswick Convention Council, England.

Cover photos: The Rev. Canon K. W. Coates, BA
(Used by kind permission.)

ISBN 1 85078 043 9

STL Books are published by Send The Light
(Operation Mobilisation), PO Box 48, Bromley, Kent,
England.

Production and printing by
Nuprint Ltd, Harpenden, Herts, AL5 4SE.

CONTENTS

The Addresses

INTRODUCTION

by Rev. Philip Hacking
(Chairman of the Keswick Convention Council)

Almost inevitably the year 1988 will go down in Keswick annals as the year the tent collapsed because of gale-force winds. But even that apparent tragedy turned to the glory of God. It gave us a marvellous opportunity to demonstrate the fellowship of 'All One in Christ Jesus' in a very practical way. The vast numbers of people who had to move location at the last minute did it with great grace and cheerfulness, which I believe will have been a witness to the town of Keswick and I know was a witness to those who came to re-erect the tent. Some of us who were called to extra commitments at the eleventh hour proved yet again the enabling of the Lord.

Any experience which throws us more upon Him can only be salutary, and therefore even the traumas of Keswick 1988 were part of the blessing.

This volume will demonstrate, I believe, the high quality of the teaching at Keswick this year. After all the excitement of our new buildings last year, we felt that we might be back to normal. Normality can be quite exciting! But there was nothing normal about the ministry of Keswick this year. There was something very practical about much of the teaching, reminding us that Christian holiness

7

is no cloistered virtue but has to be lived out in the everyday world. There was plenty of humour and this seems to be more of the ethos of Keswick today. Like everything else it needs to be kept in balance, but often the shaft of humour can drive home the Word far more than constant solemnity.

But there was serious business being done in many people's lives this year. It was indeed a real-life ministry. The two sets of Bible Readings complemented each other beautifully for those who managed the whole fortnight. Donald English opened the secrets of 1 Corinthians with a great challenge to practical unity and the working out of the compassion of the cross in everyday life. We do need to be reminded that we fight under the banner of the cross at all times and therefore there is no place for empty triumphalism. Stuart Briscoe, with his very different style in the Holiday Convention week, was equally practical with the letter of James; so that nobody could go away from Keswick with their head in the clouds. There may have been a touch of heaven, but no encouragement to a heavenly-mindedness which is no earthly use.

We rejoice this year in one or two new preachers. This is vital for the on-going work of the Convention. For the Church as a whole, as well as for Keswick, we need to discover men with a message for the hour, and there was much this year to encourage us. Not least, the Peaktime messages were very challenging to young people and everything suggested that these young people were not just being entertained but in a lively manner being taught and challenged.

This would be seen particularly in the response to the Christian Service meetings, now called World View, which happened each Wednesday morning. We do not go to Keswick just to be taught – reading sermons can perhaps give an unbalanced impression of the Convention.

Keswick is a place where we expect God to have dealings with us; and many, mostly young, men and women heard the call to commitment and responded appropriately.

If indeed we came to Keswick 1988 expecting it to be gentle and quiet after last year's opening of the new facilities and all the jamboree of the occasion, then of course we were going to be rudely surprised. But it was not just the gale-force wind that changed our thinking. There was about the whole Convention a real awareness of God at work.

It may be appropriate that the first book to be published in our new Keswick series was on the theme of mission and service. I do not think we would have planned to start that way, but again Providence took a hand. I am happy that my book on that theme started the series because ultimately the value of Keswick will be seen not just in the beauty of the setting, nor in the eloquence of the speaking, nor in the happiness of the fellowship, but in the effectiveness of real people in real-life situations once Keswick has been left behind and even a collapsing tent becomes only a memory.

Philip Hacking

EDITOR'S INTRODUCTION

As a Convention, Keswick 1988 had its unusual moments, as you will already know from the Chairman's Introduction. From an editorial point of view, we have broken a few moulds as well – chiefly in that this year the preliminary transcribing of tapes was done by STL staff who did the job in Keswick during the Convention, thereby allowing a vast army of volunteer typists, who have helped magnificently in earlier years, to have a summer holiday away from the keyboard.

However, as is the way with editing, most of this Introduction is predictable. For example, it is important to say, as we do each year, that the book is not a thoroughly revised, carefully re-written literary version of the teaching at this year's Convention. It is the transcribed, and much-edited, record of that Convention, and the speakers have graciously waived the right to scrutinise the manuscript before publication (though representatives of the Keswick Council have read it thoroughly as part of the production process).

Unlike the gardener who improves his roses by pruning, I am conscious of how much has had to be removed that was good, in order to include examples of every speaker's ministry and to keep the price affordable. For the many anecdotes, illustrations, and occasionally very funny jokes which have had to be omitted, you are recommended to make use of the excellent Keswick Tape Library mentioned elsewhere in this book. However, the substance of each message's teaching has been presented intact.

The material has been edited to preserve as much as possible of the speakers' individual styles. Bible references have been checked in the version the speaker was using at the time. Where a speaker is paraphrasing to make a point or to interpret, this is usually obvious (you are in any case recommended to have a Bible open as you read). Greek transliterations have been checked in Young's *Concordance* and other New Testament Greek handbooks.

The shape of the Keswick week, and its sequence of teaching, has been emphasised particularly in this year's volume, and though the material selected is only part of the whole ministry of the fortnight, the interplay between speakers and the way that several are often led to consider the same theme from different perspectives is especially evident this year.

David Porter

THE BIBLE READINGS:

CALLED TO BE SAINTS

by Dr Donald English

1. The Church and Its Context (1 Corinthians 1:1–17)

Laying the foundation

Let us begin by looking at the occasion of the letter to the church at Corinth. You can read the story of its founding in Acts 18:1–18a.

Paul at Mars' Hill
Paul had been on his own in Athens, as Luke tells us in Acts 17. He had become very angry at what he had found there, and had then had the opportunity to enter into a debate on the Areopagus in Mars' Hill, where he made a very interesting speech. From Athens he came to Corinth; and, as he writes in 1 Corinthians 2:2, he 'decided to know nothing amongst you except Jesus Christ and him crucified.'

Now, if you compare his speech on Mars' Hill with what he says he came to tell them at Corinth, you will find that there are some differences. If Luke gives the full account of what he said on Mars' Hill, then Paul did not mention Christ crucified.

Some have said he had found that approach unsuccessful, so he tried something different at Corinth. I don't believe that for one minute. The difference was that in

Athens he was in a debating society. So he chose from the
gospel an appropriate starting point for that audience.
When he came to Corinth, because of his own condition
('in fear and trembling') and because of the state of Corinth, he knew that the appropriate starting point for
Corinth had to be 'Christ Jesus, and him crucified'.

Paul's letters to the Corinthians

Paul's correspondence with Corinth is very complicated.
There were probably four letters, of which we have only
two. The correspondence was not very happy. Some
people at Corinth didn't think he was a real apostle, and
Paul for his part wasn't too pleased with them either. So
you will find, breaking through the two letters to Corinth
(particularly the second) a great deal of pain and hurt.
Paul tries to explain to them why he considers himself to
be an apostle, and he tries to help them to see how wrong
they are in some of the lifestyles within the church.

The purpose of the letters are twofold:

One, *he was writing to answer some of their questions*.
1 Corinthians 7:1 says 'Now for the matters you wrote
about,' so plainly they've sent him a letter, and they've
asked him some questions about things like whether
Christians should marry or not. The second reason he
wrote was that *he had heard some reports about the church
at Corinth* which didn't please him at all.

He makes an interesting reference to 'Chloe's people'.
Probably they were servants whose mistress may have
been a businesswoman, and whose 'people' were known
in that part of the world. They were plainly Christians –
whether Chloe was or not, we don't know.

So Chloe's people brought some reports, but so also did
Stephanas, Fortunatus and Archaicus about whom we
know virtually nothing. They took the letter – probably
from the church at Corinth – to Paul who was at Ephesus,

and I've no doubt they told him a thing or two about what was going on at Ephesus. So Paul has the letter from the Christians in Corinth, asking him some difficult questions about things like marriage and so on. He also has the reports from three people whom he trusts.

(And in passing, please notice this second level of leadership in the early Church. We know scarcely anything about them, yet without them Paul could not have done his work.)

The letter was written from Ephesus, probably, following the Acts chronology, in the middle of the 50s AD.

The greeting (1:1–3)

Note that Paul uses the normal form of greeting, which is to give the name of the writer, then the name of the addressee, and then some kind of greeting. Paul uses the traditional pattern, but turns it into a Christian blessing.

An incarnational and redemptive people

I ask you to pause and think about that. A very significant lesson from Paul here is this: we cannot separate ourselves wholly from our culture, nor from the developments taking place in our culture. We are a people of incarnation, and incarnation means being among the culture in which we are raised. We cannot separate ourselves, however much we would like to, because if we do we become quaint and out of date.

On the other side, we cannot wholly give ourselves to our culture. Many of the German Christians at the beginning of Hitler's regime sadly found it possible to do that, and they found themselves part of something which became an increasing horror to the world.

So we have to learn somehow to be both incarnational – those who are among the culture, and redemptive – those who are seeking all the time to redeem the culture in which they find themselves. We are in it, but we are not wholly of it.

And if we are to do this, we have to learn this lesson from Paul; that things in our culture are not always ready-made for us to use as we would like to use them. We have to discover what is there and make the most of it. If we will not do that, we will be increasingly separated from our culture, and less and less able to reach it.

That has to do with matters such as customs, words, ways of communication which are available in our culture, and the way we present ourselves in buildings, drama and – dare I say it – even music.

Things have to change in a changing world. The test is, am I incarnated in my culture in a way which enables me, by God's grace, to redeem it? John Henry Newman wasn't always wrong: he said 'to live is to change'; I believe he was right. The secret is to change redemptively.

Paul's apostleship

The greeting is from Paul, 'called to be an apostle', which means 'a sent person'. Paul puts that at the beginning, because he is going to defend his apostleship.

To be sent does not mean being sent away from God into the world, however. In Acts we often read that the Lord went ahead of them. Indeed, an important part of the missionary task as apostles is to go into the world and find out what God is doing there, and join Him. We do not take Jesus to people; Jesus, by God's grace in the Spirit, is everywhere. Our task is to discern where He is, and to witness to His presence there.

Sosthenes

Whoever is 'our brother Sosthenes'? Evidently many at Corinth knew who he was. He may well have been the

Corinthian Jew who was in charge of the synagogue (Acts 18:17); if so, he was rather an unfortunate man – he was the head of the synagogue who had to bring the case against Paul to Gallio. That didn't go too well, so the Jews in anger beat Sosthenes. Some of the texts say that the Gentiles beat him also, but if he's now Paul's colleague, he must have become a Christian, so probably the Jews beat him for becoming a Christian, and the Gentiles beat him for being a Jew. So he lost on both counts. But out of that very painful experience, here is Paul's brother; beaten for the faith, and therefore coming to believe it.

The Church of God in Corinth

There are three tensions in the Christian life indicated in this greeting. They can be life-giving or they can be destructive.

Corinth was a new Roman colony, replacing the old colony which had been razed to the ground. It was the capital of Achaia. It was a natural stopping-place on the trade routes. The Isthmian games were held nearby. It was a famous intellectual and cultural centre.

It was also an extremely confusing place; R.P. Martin describes it as a meeting place of Greek philosophy, Jewish esoteric ideas and oriental mythology.

And it was extremely wicked. The Greeks had a verb 'to Corinthianise' – 'to lead a dissolute life'. 'Corinth' formed the root for the name of a whole range of immoral activities. In the first century, to tell someone to go to Corinth was the equivalent of telling them to go to the devil. It was the place where you did not want your children to study.

Corinth's extreme wickedness was, sadly, reflected in the church. There was immorality (ch.5), law cases between Christians (ch.6), carelessness about the consciences of others (ch.8), idolatry (ch.10) and improper behaviour at communion meals (ch.11). As Moffat put it, 'The church was in the world as it had to be, but the world was in the church as it ought not to have been.'

Being the Church of God

So let me explode the myth that all the Christians in the early Church were ideal Christians. That myth takes only Paul and his friends as our antecedents. It forgets the others.

But they were, on the whole, a fairly mixed bunch just as we are. Like us they got many things wrong. If you don't believe that, read 1 Corinthians and Galatians.

The problems facing the early Church were just as serious as those facing us. Those Christians did not survive because they were better than us, they survived because they knew what the gospel was about.

So how will the church at Corinth survive as the Church of God? Simply by *being* the Church of God. Christensen points out that this is a rejection of all party spirit, of all attempts to hijack the Church for ourselves. It is the Church of God. That is why I tremble a little when I hear ministers and pastors talking about 'my' Church.

Let me just remind you of how much emphasis there is on that in this passage we're looking at.

Called to be the Church of God

Verse 1: *Called to be an apostle* – 'called' is in the active voice, a form only employed when used of God. In the New Testament, only God calls in that way – 'by the will of God'.

Verse 2: the word used for church is *ekklēsia*. This is an example of what we saw earlier. *Ekklēsia* was a secular word, not a religious one. There were Greek religious words used to describe religious gatherings, but Paul puts

them all to one side, because they're much too complicated; and he takes a purely secular word: *ekklēsia*.

It meant a gathering of people, usually on a political
basis. Paul, taking a word from his culture which had
nothing to do with religion, fed it with meaning by calling
it the *ekklēsia tou theou*, the 'Church of God'.

Do you see what I mean? He also took a very pale
word, agapē, which means 'love', and filled it with Christian meaning. Those words didn't come to him out of his
religious background, he found them in the culture and
filled them with Christian meaning.

That's what I was talking about earlier: incarnational
activity which becomes redemptive.

The emphasis continues: verse 3, 'Grace and peace . . .
from God'; verse 8, 'He will keep you'; verse 9: 'He has
called'. The whole point about the church at Corinth was
not that some people at Corinth thought, 'Wouldn't it be
nice to have a church?' It was that God said, 'I will have a
church at Corinth'. And God determined to keep it.

Set apart for God
'Sanctified in Christ Jesus and called to be holy.' Imagine
being able to say that about these folks at Corinth!

'Sanctified' is a word which comes from a root which
means 'to cut', and therefore it means to separate, to set
apart; and because the Church is set apart *for* some things,
it has to be set apart *from* others.

In the Old Testament, there were separated days, separated places, separated people, separated events, separated activities – called holy days, holy places, holy people
– and Paul says to the people at Corinth, 'You are set
apart like that.'

It's like the big black square you find on forms that you
fill in: 'For official use only'. We are for official use only!

So, 'sanctified' means that God sees even the Corinthian Christians, with all that history of bad behaviour,

as sanctified, set apart in Christ Jesus. Because their faith
is in Christ, God sees them in Christ. If you like, that is
their status before God.

There is a pun in the Greek here. The word for 'holy'
comes from the same root as the word for 'sanctified'.
Paul is saying the Church is holy, and is called to be holy.
The process of the Christian life is the process whereby
God changes us into that which He took us to be, the
moment we accepted Christ Jesus.

If you want to see that wonderfully spelled out, look at
2 Corinthians 3:18, where Paul uses the image of a mirror.
Where in a normal mirror the reflected image conforms to
your own face, the more you look at the image of Christ in
this mirror, says Paul, the more you grow to resemble
Him.

That's the process of becoming sanctified. Thank God
that when we fail, we are not dismissed! Thank God that
when the Church isn't as it might be, God doesn't say
'They're hopeless.' He says, 'I see them in Christ Jesus,
sanctified, and I will seek to help them to really be, in that
condition, what they actually are in their status before
me.' That, I think, is one of the most reassuring truths of
Scripture.

Called to be holy – and united
Thirdly, and harder for us, we are 'called to be holy
together with all those everywhere who call on the name
of our Lord Jesus Christ, their Lord and ours'. Paul means
what he says. And he is saying that the call to holiness is a
call that goes out to all those who are in Christ Jesus, who
call on the name of our Lord Jesus Christ, their Lord and
ours.

In other words, holiness is inextricably linked with
unity. Christian disunity spoils holiness and hinders our
sanctification.

John Wesley preached a sermon called 'The Catholic Spirit', one of the most unusual and unlikely texts from the Old Testament – 2 Kings 10:15 – in which he says, 'I do not ask you what are your opinions; I do not ask you what are your church practices; I do not ask you what is your moral standard; I ask you, is your heart with God as my heart is with God? If so, give me your hand.'

That, I believe, is the way to holiness. Don't neglect that little text, my sisters and my brothers who take the Bible with great seriousness.

Grace and peace

'Grace' is the Greek greeting; 'peace' (*shalom*) is the Hebrew greeting. Paul, interestingly, reverses them; he should have put peace first, because the Old Testament comes before the New. Peace (*shalom*) is not absence of war; peace is that inner state of well-being because God is in control – that's *shalom*. But Paul knows that you don't get *shalom* without grace, without peace, without God's gift to you. And so he reverses the order and he says, the grace of Jesus Christ will give you the peace for which our Old Testament forefathers were looking. As the old commentator Edwards put it, grace is the source, peace is the consummation. There is no peace without grace. That's the basis of our message.

Practical problems and theological solutions

Now he comes, strangely, to thanksgiving, in verses 4–9. This is a very practical letter about practical problems in the life of the church and *therefore* (please notice my way of putting it) it is heavily theological. The solutions to our practical problems are almost always theological solutions. And trying to deal with a church which has gone astray in all kinds of ways, Paul starts with a very strong Christology. Just notice how many times Jesus Christ is mentioned:

'Grace given in Jesus Christ' (verse 4); 'in him you have been enriched' (verse 5); 'our testimony about Christ' (verse 6); 'you eagerly await for our Lord Jesus Christ to be revealed' (verse 7); 'blameless on the day of our Lord Jesus Christ' (verse 8); 'in fellowship with his Son, Jesus Christ our Lord' (verse 9).

Now, four comments on that:

Receiving grace

It is *receiving* grace in Christ Jesus that marks out the Christian, not a particular expression of that grace. Paul says, 'You have received grace, therefore you have power, you have knowledge, you have gifts in the Spirit.'

Now the distinguishing feature in the Christian, the ground for inclusion within the circle, is that she or he receives or has received grace through Jesus Christ. The precise gift that receiving it imparts is secondary.

So any attempt to divide the Church in terms of those who have particular abilities or spiritual gifts misses the point. It turns what is secondary into what is primary. And, as I understand the New Testament, that is heresy.

Jesus the clue to creation

Jesus really does make the difference. New Testament writers say, 'He is the clue to the creation of the world' (cf. John 1, Colossians 1, Hebrews 1). They say that He is the centre of God's redemptive work, He bore our sins in His own body on the tree; they say that He is the marker for the end of all things. You can't really have more than that. He's the secret of the beginning, He's the secret of everything we have got now, and He's the secret of everything at the end.

So my sisters and my brothers, why aren't you more excited about it? How do you manage to be so dull in worship, how do you manage to look so serious, how do I manage to look so serious? This is the most exciting news in the world! That God has in a person, Jesus Christ, given us the clue to the creation of the world, the clue for the meaning of life now, and an indication as to where everything is going to go.

This is the clue to everything we are about. We are either in Jesus or we are not in Jesus, and that is the most significant question in the whole of history.

The Christian's perspective

The Christian perspective is the longest of all. As he is describing what we are now experiencing, Paul tells us to look forward eagerly to the revealing of Jesus Christ.

Theologians sometimes call this the eschatological perspective. It means that Christians who are in the kingdom see everything in the light of how it will all end. We look towards the coming of Jesus Christ, and therefore for us nothing is ever finished.

You're having hard experiences today, and you feel you will never see the way? You feel you've let the Lord down and things are in ruins? Look out, there is a long journey yet. We're still on the way to the *eschaton*, the end; we're still looking eagerly forward.

When they were told the world was coming to an end, some monks in monasteries started creating that beautiful manuscript called the Book of Kells. They spent a week over a single letter, while everyone was saying, 'Christianity is coming to an end!'

The monks replied, 'Well, yours may be coming to an end, but ours isn't! We're looking for the coming of our Lord Jesus Christ.' That's real broad-mindedness! To judge everything today in the light of what will be. Isn't that wonderful?

The unveiling of Christ

The Second Coming is not always described in the New Testament as the return of someone who has been away. Here it is 'unveiling', *apokalupsis*, which actually means the unveiling of someone who has been there all the time.

Before the unveiling of an art object or monument, many present are wondering what it will look like. But not everybody; the artist or the sculptor knows – and so does the person who commissioned it, or there wouldn't have been a ceremony!

So when the curtain is pulled back, some are able to say 'I knew it was going to be like that.'

That's the word being used here. We are moving forward towards the *eschaton*, the unveiling of our Lord Jesus Christ. And when He is unveiled, we will all say, 'That's what we've been waiting all our lives for. It's actually happened!'

And we'll look back at these little things (as they'll then seem) which are almost destroying us now, and we'll say, 'Imagine, I walked out of the church because of this or that! Imagine, I got so depressed because something happened on the TV! Imagine, because so and so was in power, I thought everything was coming to an end!'

But those around us will say, 'Did you *know* it was going to be like this?'

'Oh yes,' we'll say, 'We've known all along.'

'Well – wouldn't it have been nice to tell us? Might you not have shared that good news, so that we might not now have to run to the rocks to hide us?'

The longest view is the broadest view, it's the most healthy view, but it brings with it the most enormous responsibility to tell other people.

Grow in patience

Thanking God for difficult people

Please notice first, 'I always thank God for you' (verse 4).

The Church and Its Context   25

That was a real mark of grace in Paul, because frankly, I don't think most of us would have thanked God for this lot. They would have been an embarrassment to us!

I suspect that Paul, as so often in Corinthians, is demonstrating one of the most distinguishing features of the Christian: he is looking at life through God's eyes in Jesus Christ, not in terms of his own assessment. So he sees the Corinthians sanctified in Christ Jesus, being moved toward the *eschaton*. As one writer said, for a moment he manages to notice all the blessings they have had.

In my work I often have to deal with difficult people. I find it helpful to say, 'I wonder what he would have been like if he hadn't been a Christian?' That's what Paul is saying here. He's saying, 'Well I know they're bad, but imagine what they would have been like unredeemed!'

Receiving the grace

The second thing is that the list we have here reminds us, in Tom Smail's words, that 'Christianity is about receiving as well as about believing.' I think the Charismatic renewal has taught us that. Christianity means to receive from God, as well as to believe in God. It's not all about determining that things will be better. It's about receiving the grace that God has to give.

Enriched in every way

But thirdly, what dynamite they had received! 'They were enriched in every way.'

Our speaking

'In all your speaking' – that's the word *logos*. You remember what James had to say in James 3:5–6 about the tongue; anyone who is controlled with their tongue is probably wholly controlled.

Oh, the power of speech! It is so full of dynamic force; but if the Spirit gives you the gift of speaking, learn the discipline of handling the gift with stewardship. It's not yours to impress people, to gather great crowds, to make people say 'Wasn't he marvellous?'

The gift of speaking is one of the most dangerous gifts God can give you. Guard it, brothers and sisters, with care.

Our knowledge

The word for 'knowledge' is *gnōsis*, from which you get the word 'gnostic' which became a heresy in the second century after Christ. Gnostics always claimed an extra bit of knowledge that set them above everyone else. They were like spiritual ticket touts. The kind of people who are always tapping you on the shoulder, asking you if you know about something that no one else has ever heard about.

Sometimes it's the 'second blessing'. I remember Dr Graham Scroggie at Keswick saying, 'They say to me, "Dr Scroggie, do you believe in the 'second blessing'?" – to which I reply, "I do believe in the 'second blessing'; how else would I receive the third and the fourth and the fifth?"!'

It's not knowledge hidden by the elite, knowledge that enables us to look out on to 'all those other Christians who have never really entered into all this'. Beware gnosticism!

Knowledge from God is free, open and for everybody. The most uneducated can grasp the knowledge of God; the most learned is out of his depth in it. It's for everybody. Be glad about your knowledge! But the claims that are made in some Charismatic circles about what God is telling them to say give the impression that God has gone into His dotage. People are talking about prophecies, and words of knowledge, and special interpretations – and they're as obvious as the sun coming up in the morning, obvious to everyone who reads the Bible. But some people have to have a word of knowledge to be somebody.

Don't misunderstand me. I think all those gifts are God-given. But I'm talking about what we do with them.

Our gifts

The third word that they're given is gifts, *charismata*.

Before they were experiencing all the gifts, the Corinthians had drawn up a league table, and then they drew up a super-league table.

Beware, if God gives you exciting spiritual gifts.

There are people who are rampaging around God's Church, claiming gifts of the Spirit, like people with Sten guns in their hands, mowing everybody down. The gifts of the Spirit are *charismatic*; that's what it means. And they are *dangerous*, my sisters and brothers, unless they are held under the Word of God in Scripture, unless they are held in total obedience to Christ, unless they are held in stewardship for which we will answer.

I will look into the eyes of Christ one day for what I'm doing with this Bible study, and you will look into the eyes of Christ for what you are doing with it.

God is faithful

Gifts of God are very deep, and behind it all God is faithful (verse 9). That's the clue to everything. That's why we're here.

Why do we read Scripture? Why we believe He will bless us this time? Why do we live as Christians? Why do we say our prayers? Why do we claim His promises? Because God is faithful.

'God who calls you is faithful and he will do it' (1 Thessalonians 5:24). Brother, sister, minister, leader, teacher, in a difficult spot – God who called you is faithful;

He will do it. Sister, brother, in a difficult place of witness, at home, where everybody's against you – God who called you is faithful; He will do it. He will!

Believe it! That's the heart of what it's all about. And if people say you might be wrong, of course we might! But I'd rather be wrong this way, than right any other way. If we are right, the witness of God in Jesus says God is faithful. Jesus' way was the way of the cross, God's way was the way of resurrection. God calls us to carry the cross, and He brings about the resurrection.

The sectarian spirit

The last section is 10–17. Sadly, the sectarian spirit.

An appeal to agree with one another

Parakaleō, the word 'I appeal', means, 'I appeal to the mind'. It's used over a hundred times in the New Testament. It is an appeal to change our understanding, to change our attitudes, and Paul is saying to Christians who are divided into little groups, 'I am appealing to you to change your minds, to change your attitudes about this.'

And I think you and I, and perhaps evangelical Christians in particular, are inclined to excuse ourselves, because we have a feeling that somehow spirit is more important than, and separate from, mind. But that isn't Paul's understanding. We say, we like tradition better. We say 'Don't go confusing me with arguments, my mind is made up.' But Paul says, 'I appeal to you to change your mind, change your attitude.'

About what? 'That all of you agree with one another so that there may be no divisions among you.' It means literally, all of you speak the same thing.

Now if 'all of you' means 'all believers', which I think it does, then that commits us to work with all other believers, however misled we may think they all are; to work with them, and pray with them until we have come to think the same thing. That's what it says.

Unless, of course, you manage to solve the problem by saying, 'Only evangelical Christians are Christians' – in which case you don't need the word 'evangelical', do you?

I remember somebody praying in a prayer meeting, who said, 'Lord, we don't understand why you go on blessing the people who have got it all wrong.' It's one of the few times I have heard laughter in a prayer meeting!

But you see, it's true. God does not seem to be as fussy as we are.

Steps toward division

The first sectarian step is to ignore the theological understanding of the Church as the Body of Christ, that everyone who is in Christ belongs to the body.

The second sectarian step is to narrow the message out of loyalty to one teacher or group of teachers. That's the second step.

The third sectarian step is to give undue honour to that teacher or group of teachers, and the fourth sectarian step is to dismiss everybody else.

Now that's what they were doing in Corinth. And Paul can hardly believe it – he's heard from Chloe's household (verse 11) that one group says 'I follow Paul', another 'I follow Apollos', another 'I follow Cephas' – that's the Aramaic form of the name Peter – and another 'I follow Christ'.

It's like all those minor parties in a parliamentary by-election. The Paul Party, I'm sure, was the freedom-from-the-law party. Paul was so clear about grace over against law, that he'd got some disciples whom he didn't really want. They belonged to the Paul Party. The Apollos Party was the importance-of-the-intellect party. Apollos was from Alexandria, a brilliant preacher, good thinker; you remember that he had to be helped along by Aquila and Priscilla because he hadn't got the whole message right, but once he got it right the power of his clever preaching was tremendous. The Peter Party, or Cephas Party, was the don't-forget-our-Jewish-heritage party. Peter was a Jew who held in Jerusalem to many of the laws that the Jewish Christians brought with them. And the Christ Party was simply the we-don't-need-anybody party – 'We get our word direct from the Lord; we don't need preachers, teachers; we certainly don't need theological colleges; we certainly don't need to be taught anything – the Lord speaks directly to us.'

Can you hear echoes of those, where you live and work? I can!

Paul asks some crushing questions – 'Is Christ divided?' (verse 13). That really means, 'Is Christ cut up and parcelled out?' That's what the word means: the thing you do with a cake. Is Christ divided? Was Paul crucified for you?

How did he manage even to write that? 'Were you baptised into the name of Paul?' The name stands for the whole person – into whose name were you baptised? And the word 'into' is the strongest of the three words available, *en*, *epi* and *eis*. *Eis* means 'right into', 'plunged into'; were you plunged into the name of Paul? Or were you plunged into the name of Christ?

If you were plunged into the name of Christ, then you were plunged into the name of Christ with all the others who were plunged into the name of Christ. Everybody who's been through baptism goes through the same way, whether you sprinkle them or whether you submerge them. They're all going through the 'into Christ'.

In coming into faith in Christ and in baptism, you have actually been plunged into the same place as all the others who are believers, whoever they are; they all belong to you, and you belong to them.

And then Paul says, 'I can hardly remember who I baptised.' There was Crispus, the Jewish synagogue leader who got converted, and Gaius his host, who's mentioned at the end of Romans, and Stephanas who was the first of the converts in Achaia. 'I think that's all,' says Paul, 'I think there are only three I baptised' – not because he doesn't think baptism is important, but because that's not what he's called for. 'Christ did not send me to baptise' – remember, Jesus didn't baptise many either – 'Christ sent me to preach the gospel, not with words of human wisdom, lest the cross of Christ be emptied of its power.'

And those words 'human wisdom' and 'the cross of Christ' introduce us to the subject of our next study. Today the sun hasn't shone a lot in our passage because we're looking at some rather dismal Christians. I promise you, tomorrow, as we come to look at true wisdom and the cross of Christ, the sun will shine.

But for the moment, let's end where we started, with the gospel of our Lord Jesus Christ, in whom we have all things. Thank God!

2. The Cross and Its Meaning (1 Corinthians 1:18–2:5)

The Christians who received this letter had only this letter because most of the others hadn't even been written. So you will notice as we go through these studies that I'm keeping almost wholly to the passage, quoting from elsewhere in Scripture only when I believe Paul was doing so. It is sometimes a very good discipline to put ourselves into the place of those who received one of these letters.

If you find yourselves saying, when I make some point, 'That's not the whole story' – I agree with you entirely! But this is *part* of the story, and I am trying to tell you only what I find to be here in this passage.

So let's look at what Paul wrote.

Human wisdom and the cross of Christ

You will remember that in verse 17 Paul emphasised two phrases at the end of his argument: 'human wisdom' and 'the cross of Christ'. And it is to these that he now comes.

This passage is about the foolishness and the weakness of God. Read, if you will, verses 18–25, and let us stay for a moment with the phrase, 'the message of the cross' (1:18). It means literally 'the word of the cross', and that's a direct contrast with verse 17, 'the words of human wisdom'. That is the choice we're given in what Paul writes here.

Now, the word of the cross has two diametrically opposed results. It either becomes foolishness to those who are perishing, or it becomes the power of God to those who are being saved.

The dividing line

Notice, first, that these are present participles: those who *are perishing*, those who *are being saved*. For those who are perishing, it is not too late to hope and pray; for those who are being saved, we have no grounds for complacency. Let him (or her) who thinks he stands, take heed lest he fall.

And I remember Bishop John Robinson, Bishop of Woolwich (who doesn't get a very good press in evangelical circles) lecturing on Romans when I was at Cambridge just beginning to study theology. I remember him saying: the dividing line in human experience is not between those who are alive and those who are dead. It runs between those who are in Christ and those who are not in Christ, and it runs straight on out into eternity.

If you go to conferences on evangelism, be careful lest you enjoy them. We are talking about those who are perishing.

Human wisdom (1:19)

The Old Testament, says Paul, is on my side (verse 19). You may recognise that he is quoting from Isaiah 29:13, and to understand what Paul means when he talks of the wisdom that is destroyed, we need to consider that passage for a moment.

What's wrong with the wisdom of the people in Isaiah 29? Well, it's quite clear, says Paul. They go through the

rituals of worship, they say all the right things, but they're
not, deep down, committed to God (Isa. 29:13). This kind
of wisdom imagines (Isa. 29:15) that God, somehow,
doesn't see what is happening. It virtually discounts Him.
And so, verse 16, they turn things upside down, as if the
potter were thought to be like the clay!

Their so-called wisdom is centred upon humans, not
God; and therefore 'the wisdom of the wise will perish,
the intelligence of the intelligent will vanish' (Isa. 29:14).
So God is going to put on one side all human wisdom that
assumes men and women to be the centre of the universe.
Where salvation is concerned, He rejects it. It is useless
for His purposes.

Back to 1 Corinthians. Verse 20 also comes from the
Old Testament, from Isaiah 33:18f. Isaiah the prophet is
talking about the Assyrians who have been controlling
Jerusalem. They have now gone home.

Of course, the leaders in Jerusalem tried to be wise
according to human wisdom. But they should never have
been there in the first place. They entered into an alliance
with Egypt; it was disastrous, they should never have done
it. Because of their alliance with Egypt, the Assyrians
took over Jerusalem. And things were in a a very bad way.

So the Assyrians had to go, and now Isaiah is having
some fun. 'In your thoughts you will ponder the former
terror' – that's the Assyrians – 'Where is that chief officer,
where is the one who took the revenue, where is the one
in charge of the towers? You will see those arrogant
people no more.' (Isa. 33:18–19.)

Wise men, scholars, philosophers, the debaters of this
world, are like the Assyrians. If you want to talk about
salvation, they are nowhere to be seen, for the simple
reason that they have nothing to offer.

But why have they nothing to offer?

Plan A and Plan B?

The reason is given in verse 21 of Paul's letter. It's not an easy verse. It could mean God had plan A and plan B. Plan A was that the world emits so many signals of His presence, the world is so redolent of God among us, that men and women should be able to perceive and receive the signals of His presence. That was God's plan A. Plainly, they couldn't, or wouldn't, and certainly didn't, so God goes to plan B, which is, Jesus Christ, incarnate, crucified, risen and ascended.

Now, I think there are two very serious obstacles in the way of that:

The first is that Paul says *it was in the wisdom of God that men and women by wisdom did not know Him*. Somehow, it was God's understanding from the beginning that human wisdom would not perceive His presence.

If you think about it, it is obvious. Everything that makes sense according to sound worldly wisdom does not make sense when you move it to the area of salvation. For example: if you do wrong to your neighbour, you have to put it right. But if you stand guilty before God, there is no way you can remedy matters by yourself. Again: if you commit a crime against your neighbour, you must bear the punishment. But if you stand as a guilty sinner before God, you need not bear the punishment, for Jesus has borne it for you.

How could men and women by wisdom perceive the presence of God when He stands all human values on their heads? So there can't have been a plan A which meant that if you think hard, and work it out, you will perceive God.

And the other obstacle of course *is that the people in the Old Testament who get most praise are not those who worked according to human wisdom*.

Moses didn't work according to human wisdom when God sent him to do what He sent him to do. He had a

stammer. But God said, 'Moses, you're the spokesman.'
It was nonsense: how could he be a spokesman with a
stammer?

'I'm not going to tell you where you are going, but don't
worry, it will be all right.' Can you imagine, gathering all
your family of three generations and setting off? 'Don't
you know where we are going, Grandad?' – 'No idea.'

'Noah, why are you building that ark in the middle of
the country? I mean, you'll never get it to the water.'

Gideon a soldier? That was a joke! He was the youngest
son of the poorest father in the whole area round about.

Do you see what I am trying to say? The people in the
Old Testament who knew God were not the people who
worked according to worldly wisdom. They were the
people who said, 'It doesn't make any sense at all, but I
believe.'

'Abram believed God, and it was counted to him as
righteousness.' So there wasn't a plan A and a plan B;
there has always only ever been one plan.

Salvation through Jesus Christ
Which was, that God would save those who believe
through Jesus Christ.

How could Abraham and Moses and the others be
saved through Jesus Christ if Jesus Christ came later?

Paul, I believe, gives us the answer here. The cross of
Jesus Christ, thank God, is wholly historical. It happened
at one time in history, once for all. But it is also a demonstration for all time, of how God has always been. It is, as
it were, the opening of the curtains of heaven, and the
lowering down of the stage on which Jesus Christ plays out
the divine drama: that God has always been 'forgiving
through Jesus Christ God'.

Therefore, Abraham, who had never heard of Jesus,
believed and found salvation because Jesus is a revelation

of the being of God. We know nothing about God with confidence, except what is revealed through Jesus Christ. I ask you to hold that in your minds, because of what is coming.

The Jews and the Gentiles

Well, what does the world make of that? 'God was pleased through the foolishness of what was preached to save those who believe' (verse 21).

The foolishness of what was preached is that God has revealed Himself wholly to us in a baby born out of bounds, in a rabbi who gathered a few people around Him who ran away at the most important time, a teacher who ended up on a cross, who His followers allege was alive three days later, and who has been with them through the Spirit evermore.

What does the world make of that? Look at verse 22. *The Jews demand miraculous signs*. They were a down-to-earth people. Hebrew idiom makes everything as concrete as possible. Leon Morris says, 'a crucified Messiah is a contradiction in terms.' The fact that Jesus was crucified meant to the Jews that there was no way that He could be the Messiah. What they wanted was external and indubitable manifestations of the power of God in Christ. They wanted another King David. And Jesus plainly was not that.

What did the Greeks make of it? The Gentiles? They thought it to be nonsense. They were a highly speculative people, they honoured the wise, they loved philosophers and their ideas. Anything not self-evidently wise did not deserve respect, especially if it was supposed to do with the divine.

'But we preach Christ crucified'

So Jews didn't like it, Gentiles didn't like it, 'but we preach Christ crucified'. The *we* is very strong in the Greek text.

They're a new people coming into being don't you see? Not Jews, not Gentiles, *we*. And what do we do? We preach Christ crucified.

Literally, 'we herald Christ crucified'.

Heralds are very important people. Firstly, the heralds of the first century went before the king announcing that he was coming.

Secondly, they went into the city-state, announcing that there was to be an assembly of citizens, and those who responded to the appeal formed the assembly. And the Greek word for assembly is *ekklēsia*. We herald Christ in order to call together the assembly, the *ekklēsia*, the Church.

Thirdly, the herald went around the games, calling the athletes to perform, and telling them what the rules were.

It was not the herald's job to invent the message. Heralds who had new ideas about how to tell it were sacked immediately. A herald's message is to tell the message as it is given.

So if Paul is, as I believe he is, using this word deliberately, we had better look out. Because it means the cross of Christ, a crucified Saviour, is the basis of the Kingdom of God.

Who is the King? The crucified One. Notice, I am not saying the 'crucified and risen One', because Paul doesn't say that. The King is the crucified One. Who are those who assemble round Him? Those who respond to the message of a crucified King. What shall be our response; how shall we become the athletes in this race? By faith alone. In what? In whom? In a crucified King. The Kingdom, the Church and Christian activity all depend on a crucified Saviour.

'Crucified' in this verse is a perfect participle. The perfect tense in Greek refers to something which happened at a particular time whose effects continue to this day. So

Christ crucified means someone crucified at one point in time, the results of which are still with us to this day.

A stumbling block and foolishness
No wonder the others didn't like it! 'A stumbling block to Jews' – they didn't just think it was weak, they thought it was offensive, for reasons given in Deuteronomy 21:23 and Galatians 3:13.

The word 'stumbling block' has its origins in the word from which we get our word 'scandal'. The fact that you would even give honour to a person who had been crucified on a tree was something they tripped over. 'You are saying the one who was hung on the tree at Calvary is the *Messiah*?' They didn't just think that was weak. They were hopping mad about it, and no wonder.

To the Gentiles it was just nonsense. Lucian talks about that 'gibbeted sophist', Jesus. And on the walls of the Palatine, there are graffiti which show a body on a cross with a donkey's head, and a slave kneeling before it. The inscription says: 'Alexaminos worships his God.' That's what the wise Greeks thought about it.

Let me ask you, have you ever tried a crucified king on any of the people who are moving in the areas of power in our culture? Just try it on the media people. Try it on the great philosophers, try it on the great politicians: 'Our king is a crucified teacher . . .'

Just watch their faces. If they are polite, they will say, 'Mmmm, yes.' But if they are honest they will say either, 'Don't trouble me with this nonsense', or 'What a joke'. Like Paul, we must go into the world taking seriously the rejection of what we are about.

To those who are called
Verse 24 enables me to say that whether we are Calvinists or Arminians, we are all agreed that the primacy in terms

of our conversion is the initiative and activity of God. We would not be Christians but for God's primacy and initiative, however we understand the response.

And the point Paul is trying to make is that while Jews go their way, and Gentiles their's, Christians are trying to go God's way.

'O my brother Jews,' he explains, 'what has happened to us is not of our choosing. It is what God has done. And you Gentiles who don't understand Jews anyway, but do believe in God – What has happened to us is not of our choosing, it is God's doing.'

And which of us does not look back and say, 'When I came through the door, I thought it said "Whosoever will may come", so I came; but when I looked back, it said "You have not chosen me, but I have chosen you"'?

It is mystery. And Paul says: make no mistake about it, if you're in the Kingdom, you're in the Kingdom because God has been good to you. So, he is saying, all we have to offer to Jews who want signs, to Greeks who want wisdom, to Jews who think it's offensive, to Greeks who think it's silly – all we have to offer is Christ crucified and herald it.

The foolishness and weakness of God

There is a very significant change in direction at this point. These letters were not originally broken up into chapters and verses as they are now, so the people reading the letter may perhaps have gasped a little when they came to what we call verse 25.

For Paul seems to concede the case of the opposition. His forbears the Jews would not even use the name of God. But now, having been rebutting the Jews and the Gentiles, he goes on to use words like the 'foolishness' and 'weakness' of God. And these are strong words in Greek.

So now Paul is admitting that the cross of Christ is foolish and weak.

If you think about the story, you will see how true that is. Imagine trying to establish a kingdom by getting the kind of followers Jesus called. Imagine trying to announce the kingdom by getting yourself killed. Nobody in their right mind would do that! Imagine the humility of not being strong enough to carry your own cross. Imagine the humiliation of looking around the crowd and hearing them baying for your death, and not being able to see the face of one of your male disciples.

Maybe John was in the crowd, the rest had gone. Some women were there, but you know the status of women in the first century. That's foolish. That's weak.

But, says Paul, this is the curious thing: the foolishness and weakness of God is evidently the way people get saved (verse 21). The foolishness of God saves people; the wisdom of men does not. The weakness of God saves people; the strength of men and women does not.

'Isn't that a joke?' says Paul. 'If I admit to you that God is at His weakest and His most foolish on the cross?' – but that is the way that people get saved for eternity.

And all your philosophers, your politicians, your sociologists don't do that. Nor your psychologists, nor your psychiatrists – and so it goes on; none of them can save a man or woman. By your arguments, says Paul, they are all evidently wiser and stronger than God.

But not all the armies of the world could save a single soul. And God, at His most foolish, offers salvation for all! 'How about that?' says Paul.

Now, my sisters and my brothers, I want to ask you whether deep down, you believe all this? I don't mean, do you feel better by believing it. I mean, do you believe it deep, deep down?

God's foolishness and weakness on the cross are His strategy for saving the world. No one comes to salvation except through the crucified Saviour. So He, through whom we reach salvation, into whom, as Paul said in our previous study, we are plunged – He is the one in whom we believe at the focal point of God's greatest weakness, God's greatest foolishness.

God's sovereignty seen in compassionate love

The next step is this: the wisdom of God decreed that He would be known in His essence in Jesus Christ; that, if you want to know what God is really like, the only place to look is Jesus Christ. If Jesus Christ is the King whom we herald then the kingship we are looking at is the kingship of the foolish, weak, crucified One.

Now, how is that God, foolish and weak in the crucified King who reveals Him, sovereign over all the world?

He is sovereign over all the world as suffering, compassionate love. That's how God is sovereign – suffering, compassionate, love. That's what Jesus revealed, wasn't it? Born in a cave, of a mother who wasn't married; raised in the far part of the Roman Empire; a rag-tag set of disciples; crowds who sometimes followed Him and ate the bread He gave them but sometimes shouted 'Crucify Him'; disciples who never really grasped it, and who ran away; a borrowed grave. That's how God is sovereign – He is crucified, compassionate love in the world.

So maybe many of our triumphalistic pictures of God have come from the wrong place. They've come from the Syrian Empire; they've come from the world's kings; they're based on Charlemagne, on Henry V, on the great monarchs, they're based on the Russian royal family – people who said 'go' and they ran; people who said 'they don't matter' and they didn't. And we want a king like that because it feels good to have a king like that. We want a king who's always got a trump card under his sleeve.

I have to tell you, I don't think that's the King of the Bible. The God of the Bible reveals His sovereignty in suffering, dying love. That's why Jesus said if somebody hits you on the cheek, don't hit him back; say, 'Would you like to hit this side?' If somebody takes your shirt, don't say, 'Give it back' – say, 'Would you like a jacket?' If somebody says, 'Carry this bag a mile,' don't say, 'Ooh, I hate carrying bags a mile – especially for Romans!' – say, 'Why one mile? Why don't I carry it two?'

Why didn't Jesus do that? Why didn't He defend Himself? He could have confused them all. Why didn't He call down the angels? They were all there; I'm sure they were all on red alert!

Because that isn't how God is sovereign.

God is love

Now, here's the next step. Suppose God exercises that kind of sovereignty because that's actually how God *is*. Suppose His sovereignty isn't just another strategy; suppose our God *is* compassionate love? What about that?

Suppose these myths that we have of a great triumphalist monarch who waves his hand and things happen are not a true picture of God? Suppose He's just compassionate love? And suppose therefore that the world is made according to God's character, so that the only way to be happy in the world is the way of compassionate love?

If you think about it a bit you will see what I'm talking about. In the world we have relationships, we have sexual relationships, we have abilities that we can use, we have money we can possess. The moment you take those as possessions they're like the second helping of manna in the wilderness – it goes rotten on you.

The moment you say, 'Ah – sex, the people who work for me, money, a good mind – they're there for my use!', they rot from the moment you grab them. From the moment you try to exploit them, they rot, because the world is made to respond to compassionate love.

And so of your abilities you say, 'How may I use these abilities to serve my sisters and my brothers?' Of relationships, you say not 'How can I get the most out of these?' but 'How can I put most into these relationships?' Of those you love, you say not 'How can I get them all running around me so that they're doing what I want?' but 'How can I meet their needs?'

Do you see? That is what God is like. But so many of us live differently. We fall out with other people and what do we do? We make nuclear bombs!

We all want to be free. 'I'm going to be free in this world. I'm going to be developed.' I hate theories of self-development for Christians. I think they are a nonsense. We all want to be developed, we all want to be fulfilled. Jesus said, 'You want to be fulfilled? Give yourself away. You want to be happy? Don't try to be happy. Happy are the poor in spirit, happy are the peace-makers, happy are those who seek righteousness.'

Why? Because happiness is a by-product of true character. Why? Because that is how God is. The world is a mirror-image of God in its original creation.

Every time you follow after these triumphalistic models, you're on the wrong track, even if you try to use them for the glory of God. Because God isn't like that.

Now, you are saying, what are the implications of that?

Love in service

Well, let's start with some of our most personal problems. How many of us in this tent have not said, 'Why doesn't God punish . . .?' 'Why doesn't God make people do . . .?' 'Why doesn't God solve *my* problem?'

A monarch could solve it instantly. He could send somebody in a car, and that person would send your oppressor to prison, or give you the money you needed, or do whatever you wanted. But God isn't like that. He doesn't behave like that.

Here is another implication. What does the gospel have to say to the majority of people in the world, who are poor and starving and needy, who are unhappy, and miserable, and in pain? What have we got to say to that? 'I am H-A-P-P-Y'?

What we have got to say to that is: 'My God suffers like that; the cross is the only place where any being has ever understood what you are going through right now.' We're the only ones with a message to the poor and the needy and the starving, because we are the only ones who worship a God who has gone that way.

But triumphalism says: 'Even if you're poor, send five pounds to me, and I'll pray for you on my holy hill, and you will be amazed at what will happen! You will be a millionaire in a month!' You laugh at that, but you can find versions of it in your own thinking. We'd all love a God like that.

And what is the message to the powerful and the privileged? It is, 'Watch out, because you're on a track which could damn your soul for eternity.' The powerful and the privileged find it so hard to learn that God is loving compassion; and if we will not speak that word, who will?

And what does this say about the role of the Church in the world?

Evidently, we are not to be the ruling majority, but to be the suffering, servant community. The test of the Church should be that wherever there are needy people in the world, you will find a Christian. That wherever there is any kind of injustice, you will find a Christian group saying, 'God, my Father, does not wish this injustice, and we are offering ourselves in order that this might be put right.'

That's what Jesus did, isn't it? 'Who, being equal with God, thought not equality with God a thing to be snatched at, grasped at, clutched; but humbled Himself, made Himself of no reputation, even to the cross' – we're back here again – 'wherefore God has highly exalted Him' (Phil. 2:9).

But Jesus' way was the way down, not the way up. It is a scandal that we Christians sleep so happily and comfortably in the midst of a needy world, when our Saviour is the Saviour who walked among the poor and the outcast and the under-privileged and went to a cross just like one of them.

So that's the clue to where He is in the world. He will be where the poor and needy are. That's where He always was. He hadn't time for many of the other parties, because He was too busy with the outcasts.

That is why we must 'continue to work out our salvation with fear and trembling' (Phil. 2:12). The eyes you look into at the end of the road are the eyes of endlessly loving compassion. Imagine looking into those eyes and admitting how shallow you've been. A threatening God is one thing. But a God who looks at you out of the eyes of the crucified Saviour and says, 'And is *that* how you lived?' is far more to be feared.

A Church that is as loving and compassionate as God is, can never be effectively persecuted. I know that in my garden it's the weeds that don't resist me, the ones that allow themselves to be pulled up and broken, that are quietly renewing themselves below ground. And the person who says, 'Did you hit me on the cheek? – Try this one! A mile? Let's walk two miles. Anything else?' – how do you persecute that?

It doesn't claim anything, it doesn't possess anything. It all belongs to the loving compassionate God whose Son said to the Father, 'I'd really rather not go through with this; but if this has got to be the way, I'm in!'

We need to revise many of our views of God – particularly as they work out in the life of the Church. You may say to me, 'Of course there was a cry of dereliction on the cross, but wasn't there also a cry of triumph?'

Though Paul is not speaking about that here, let me take up that point. What was the cry of triumph on the cross? 'It is finished!'

What was finished? The way of suffering, dying love was finished. He didn't say, 'It's coming', meaning the resurrection, He said 'It's finished'. Resurrection was God's work. Jesus' task was the Gethsemane road to Calvary. Paul says in Romans 1 that Jesus is declared to be the Son of God with power by His resurrection from the dead. He doesn't say, 'God had a trump card up His sleeve!' He's saying, 'The way Jesus went is the right way.'

He did not think equality with God something to be clutched at, but humbled himself, becoming lowly even to the cross. And then, says Paul in Philippians, God takes over: 'wherefore has God highly exalted Him, and given Him a name above every name'.

You see, we all want the resurrection, but not via the cross. But God says, you leave the resurrection to me, you look after the cross bit. Jesus did not say 'Believe in the cross, adore my cross!' He said, 'Carry your cross.' Too many of us are on the resurrection trail, but we don't want to go by way of a cross.

I spoke in Nairobi at the World Methodist Council. A white woman, I would guess very well off, came to me on the platform after I had spoken. With tears in her eyes she said, 'I have discovered today listening to you what I must do back in South Africa. I must ignore the culture in which I have been raised, and reach out to the black people in need. And that is my way of dying with Christ. And I have to trust God with the resurrection.'

My sisters and my brothers, that's meant to be our daily experience. We are meant daily to die into Christ, that we might rise with Him. And that is a risk you take every day, in every step of the Christian life, if you follow that kind of God.

But you see, it's so liberating! This is the sun that is shining, because this way, the world can't do anything to us. It can't threaten us. What will it take from us? We don't have anything. What will it do to us that we fear? Nothing, because we are dead in Christ already. Will we be on the losing side? We will never be on the losing side, because the suffering compassionate love in God will always be stronger than anything else in the world or in eternity.

That's what Paul says in Romans 8. That's why the message of Christ crucified does what wisdom and power in the world cannot do.

And just in closing, because it illustrates beautifully, verse 26: 'Brothers, think of what you were when you were called.' In other words – if you don't believe this, look around you. Look at yourselves! If God was a God who had a court with nobility, why would you be sitting in the fellowship? How did you get in?

Are any of you, he says, wise by human standards? Many influential? Many of noble birth? Well, look around! God chose the foolish, weak, lowly things of the world to shame the wise, He chose the despised things and the things that are not to nullify things that are, so that no-one may boast before Him. It's not that the noble and the wise and the strong are excluded; it's just that they won't get in through being noble and wise and strong. God chooses that way, in order to show that the gospel is His, and not ours, so that no-one may boast before Him.

I think that goes back to Jeremiah. Out of all the prophets, poor Jeremiah had least to boast about. He hated being a prophet. He said, 'Lord, please don't send me any more of those messages, I really can't tell them anything. They'd throw me into holes, or they'd beat me, or my family throws me out. Don't tell me any more.' So God says, 'All right, Jeremiah.' But Jeremiah is simply burning with his message, he has got to tell it.

'So that no one may boast' except in the Lord, because in Christ Jesus, we have all the wisdom we need. Verse 30: 'righteousness' – *dikaiosunē*, the word Paul uses in Romans to mean that Jesus has put us in the right; 'holiness', which we saw yesterday means becoming like Jesus as we look into the mirror; and 'redemption', which here means the whole completed story when we get to glory.

'Therefore, as it is written, let him who boasts boast in the Lord.' I find this one of the most moving passages of Scripture. To think that our God is loving compassion, reaching out to the whole wide world, is at once both inspiring and humbling. And that is the sun that shines for ever.

3. Wisdom and Its Secret
(1 Corinthians 2:6–16)

Today we're dealing with a single word, and that word is 'wisdom'.

Last time I didn't finish the passage that I was promising to deal with, so we look very briefly at 1 Corinthians 2: 1–5 this morning, as a run-in to the topic of wisdom from verse 6 onwards. Since Paul didn't write in chapters and verses, you can do this kind of thing without feeling too guilty about it.

There are three things that Paul is trying to make plain in these verses, about the first time he came to them in Corinth.

1. *The testimony that he bore was to Jesus Christ and Him crucified*. That is the message he came with; that is what he intended them to hear; that is what he told them; and it was to that which they responded.

2. *But what he said was said in the demonstration of the Spirit's power*. And that is by contrast with what is translated in the NIV as 'eloquence' or 'superior wisdom'. 'Superior wisdom' means literally 'the word of wisdom', and the expression is used primarily when discussing speaking technique, of which there was a great deal in the first century. Paul says, 'I had a choice between con-

centrating on the content or concentrating on the method, and I was so frightened anyway, I couldn't have produced a method if I tried. So in weakness and in trembling I simply told you about Christ crucified. If anything resulted from my telling you, it cannot have been on the basis of my technique but only because God's Spirit was at work.'

3. *He expected a faith response, and that's what happened.* 'So that your faith might not rest on men's wisdom but on God's power.'

The question, of course, is this. If you have spoken in such a deprecating fashion about the rulers, the nobility, and the wise; and if you have dismissed in a sentence the requests of the Jews for signs and the Gentiles for wisdom – are you saying that there is no place for wisdom in the Christian faith? Paul wishes to deny that emphatically. There is room for wisdom among Christians, he says; and that's what he comes to in our passage today.

A wisdom among the mature

Paul makes clear, in chapter 2 verse 6, that when he is dismissing worldly knowledge he is dismissing it purely in the area of salvation. He's not saying that there's anything wrong with studying mathematics, or being a philosopher, or a politician – as long as you don't expect to be saved by mathematics, or philosophy, or politicians' words.

Of course it is perfectly acceptable to use, in everyday life, the wisdom that comes from intellectual study. But we are talking about salvation. And where that is concerned, those things don't fit in. But there is a wisdom that attaches to Christianity that depends upon the gospel, that is known among the mature – *teleioō*.

Teleioō, translated here in the plural, is used of an animal or a person that is fully grown, or of people who have completed a required course of study. It is, I think, used here in contrast to *nēpios* in 3:1, which is translated in the NIV 'mere infants'. In 14:20 you'll find both words used in the same verse.

So, Paul is saying, there is a wisdom in the Christian faith. It's not a wisdom which babes in Christ should be expected to understand, but it is a wisdom which the mature in Christ should be expected to understand.

May I take a little time now, to explain some very complicated use of words in the next few verses.

Three kinds of Christian

Paul seems to be categorising Christians into three groups. The first he describes as *teleioō*, mature, or (verse 15) *pneumatikos*, the spiritual person. So one set of Christian attitudes he is calling adult and spiritual; there is a wisdom you would not expect in babies, but you should expect it in adults.

The second group is found in 3:1. They're either worldly, *sarkikos*, or *nēpios*, infants. Of this group Paul says that because of their stage of development, we can't expect them to grasp the wisdom he's about to describe. Still worldly, so recently come into the faith that they've brought a whole lot of worldly baggage with them. They haven't been able to get rid of that yet. How could they? So don't expect of them what they're not yet able to develop.

Then there's the third group. The worrying ones. In 3:3 he describes them as 'worldly', which looks in translation to be the same word as in verse 1, but it isn't. It's a slightly different form. So I want to translate that 'fleshly worldly' or, also in 3:3, 'acting like mere men'.

Now, the trouble with that group is that, unlike the first two, they oughtn't to be like that. They've been in the faith a long time, but they're still fleshly worldly; they're still thinking like men and women in the world.

Growth and its consequences

There are two conclusions to be drawn from what Paul is saying. The first is, that Paul is underlining the fact that *the Christian faith is a process of growth*.

He's not locking people away in groups and saying, 'Of course, they're *only* this kind of Christian.' He's saying that there are 'professional' Christians, the kind Alistair Begg was warning us of in his address[1] – that most Christians will never get that far, you can't expect much from them?

No! He is saying there is a process, a progress, in the Christian life; and that it is the task of preachers and teachers to bring all the babies to maturity. And the test of your preaching and mine, my brother and sister preachers and teachers, is this: 'Is it bringing the babies right though to maturity? Or are there people whom I preach or teach who are stuck – happy to be where they are, not growing? Is my preaching so predictable that it will never take anybody anywhere?'

The pattern that Paul is talking about here is the pattern that I referred to earlier in 2 Corinthians 3:18. We are all meant, looking into the mirror that gives us the reflection not of our faces but of Christ's, to be becoming like the image we see in the mirror. We are meant to be becoming like Christ. We need to ask ourselves, where am I now in terms of my Christian growth?

The second point I think is more searching and more difficult, and it is this: *Those of us who have been Christians for a long time, and might be described by-and-large as mature, are all capable of these other attitudes*. We are all capable of becoming *teleioō, nēpios, sarkikos*.

For example, the prominent Christian who at conferences was always known for the time he spent alone in prayer, but usually spent it in places where most of the rest of the conference could see him praying. That's *sarkikos*, that's worldliness.

I believe that many of us who are mature are liable to fall into such attitudes, become children again, when we're prodded in unexpected places. And therefore the challenge, if you think of yourself as mature, is to watch out for the baby in you who keeps bursting out again. If you think there is nothing like that in your life, ask your spouse, or somebody else who knows you well, and you'll get the answer very quickly!

Keswick has never been about a plateau on to which you get, where for ever afterwards you're in a different class from everybody else. The emphasis has always been on the daily total commitment, which means that maturity becomes more and more a reality and we're constantly looking for those new areas where the baby has to grow up. I can't tell you what your areas are, but somebody who knows you could!

Living in two worlds

'But not the wisdom of this age or of the rulers of this age, who are coming to nothing.' Let me spend some time expounding this 'age', which I think is very helpful in trying to understand what this passage is all about.

In the New Testament there are two ages described. One is often called 'this present evil age', and the other the 'age to come'. 'This present evil age' began with the fall of men and women into sin. And it goes right on through to the end of the world. That's this present evil age.

All worldly thinking and worldly activity belongs to it. It started with the entry of sin in the world, and ends with the end of the world. But into this present evil age, at a particular point in time, Jesus Christ was born, and with the coming of Jesus began 'the age to come'. The two ages run parallel to each other until the end of the world, but then the age to come runs on, out into eternity.

We are living, you and I, my brothers and sisters, in the overlap. And the business of being sanctified is the business of being moved from this present evil age into the age to come while still living in the overlap. That's why it's difficult to be a Christian who is growing, and why it's easy for any mature Christian to slip back again to the old way.

Now, Paul says, get it absolutely clear: which world do you wish to belong to? And whatever you do, don't keep hopping from one to the other. The two ages are parallel, but they're not going in the same direction. Therefore you must ask yourself, which age do I really want to belong to?

Neither the wisdom of this age, nor the rulers of this age, understand this wisdom; because this wisdom is related to crucified Christ, and we've already heard that they don't understand it. There is no future, in salvation terms, for the wisdom of this age.

No, 'We speak of God's secret wisdom.' The word is the one from which we get the English word 'mystery' – it occurs a number of times in this letter, in 4:1; 13:2; 14:2; 15:51. Mystery here doesn't mean what we mean when we say, 'It's all very mysterious.' It's not the perplexing mystery of the magician's skill. 'Mystery' means 'once hidden but now revealed'.

What is it that was once hidden but now revealed? Of course, the answer is that God is saving those who believe through the death of Jesus Christ.

A mystery revealed

The 'wisdom that has been hidden and that God destined for our glory before time began.' Isn't that wonderful? That suffering, compassionate love was always going to be God's way of saving those who would believe, and it was planned before the beginning of time so that we – that is, those who believe – might experience that glory.

'Glory' always means the revealed presence of Christ. 'None of the rulers of this age understood it, for if they had, they would not have crucified the Lord of glory.' Who are the rulers of this age? Some commentators think Paul means primarily principalities and powers. I don't think so myself; I think he means those who crucified the Lord of glory. And the awful thing about that is that it was both the secular rulers and the religious leaders who crucified the Lord of glory. Of course the principalities and powers were behind it, but both the secular and religious leaders – the religious leaders being His own equals – crucified the Lord of glory, because they were not willing to accept that salvation is purely by the death of Jesus Christ on our behalf.

I simply raise the question to trouble all of us who are in leadership: how often are discussions in churches dominated by something other than this principle of the loving, crucified love of God being the redemptive agency of mankind? We're so often into other thought forms – triumphal thought forms; power thought forms; thought forms of dominance; imperialistic thought forms; thought forms which neglect other people and their concerns; thought forms which don't try to understand other people and *their* thought forms; evangelism which tries to start where we are and not where they are; judgements passed about young Christians who can't possibly deliver what we expect of them; I could go on.

Paul said, that's the sort of thing that crucified the Lord of glory. So my brothers and my sisters, let us beware.

So what is this wisdom? Well, *it's in Christ*. That's point one. Two, *it's now revealed*, which must be a reference to Christ crucified, who he's been talking about in this letter. Three, *it has something to do with the rulers of this age*, otherwise this reference wouldn't have any point to it at all. That is, it may be fundamentally about how you and I find our salvation in Jesus Christ, but Paul is already hinting that it also has something to do with the way the government should be governing, as well as the way in which religious leaders should be leading.

So it's getting to be a bit broader now. It's not just for the newly converted, so it's got to be something wider than what we call the 'simple gospel'. And yet it is directly related to it. It's not a separate, self-contained package; it grows out of the simple gospel.

Well now, what can all that be?

The scope of the gospel

I think Paul is saying this: that all you need in order to *become* a Christian is to know that Jesus Christ was crucified for you, and to give your life to Him in response. Thank God, that's all the babies need to know! But the question that faces you the moment you *are* a Christian is: How am I going to live out in daily life what it means to have given myself to God in Jesus Christ? What does it mean to be a disciple within the Church? That's where this wisdom starts to work out – the spiritual secrets of being a Christian.

And then, what does it mean to live at home as a Christian? That's another bit of the wisdom that has to be learned. And what does it mean to be at work as a Christian? – It's the wisdom that has got to be learned. And then, bit by bit, you begin to discover that it's not 'I', it's 'we'. When you come to Jesus it's highly individualistic. But before long you discover that it's not just a matter of 'I'; it's about 'we'. And therefore this wisdom is not just about how I may come to Jesus, through Jesus to God, it's about how I may belong to the Body of Christ.

The wisdom is about how I relate to you, and how you relate to me.

And then, as I look out at my home, and at my work, I begin to think, 'This can't be individualistic either; this has to take on board the shape of my family, the shape of

those with whom I work,' – and that's where this wisdom
begins to apply. And all the time you're saying, 'How does
the simple gospel – God's love for the world which was
revealed in suffering, compassionate love which Jesus
demonstrated in dying, and then God raised Him from the
dead – how does that apply to the Body of Christ, to the
life of my family, to what's going on at work?' Then I have
to say that God who sent Jesus Christ is the God of all the
world. So how does God's suffering compassionate love in
Jesus Christ relate to what's going on in the world?

Now I'm into politics, economics, sociology, psychology, national relationships, international relationships!
And the question is still the same question: 'How does the
gospel, revealed in a suffering, crucified Saviour whom
God raised from the dead – how does that apply to all of
that?'

Speaking from maturity

This is the wisdom that Paul is talking about, that belongs
to the mature. Now, how many of you feel mature? How
far have you got from being a baby who needs to sit having
your hand held? How far have you launched out into the
application of the gospel – not just to your life, not just to
your family, not just to your work, but to all those you
meet in those circumstances? And how far have you got
beyond that – I mean, what have you to say out of the
centre of the gospel about unemployment? What have you
to say out of the centre of the gospel about the poor in our
nation? What have you to say about the economic system
that is built on growth of wealth so that those who are
most able will make most? Have you anything to say
about that?

Don't tell me, 'That's politics.' I'm talking about gospel
– gospel relating to people. And if God is the God of all
the world, all of that must matter infinitely to Him. The

truth of the matter is, there are hardly any of us who are mature. And we're not mature because we're too lazy to be mature, or we're too afraid to be mature, because it's better just to sit in our little churches and chapels, having a Bible study and a prayer meeting, and saying about the news, 'I don't know what we're coming to!' – or blaming other people for what we're coming to.

But by and large, this country has come to what *we* have allowed it to come to. We are responsible, largely, as Christians for the way this country has slid in all directions. Don't blame the Government, don't blame the media, don't blame the newspapers, don't blame the pop stars. We are the ones who are guilty. We have kept in our little chapels while the world has slid away from Christ, and we have made it a wholly individualistic thing, and we've no consecutive comment to make about all these great issues. And then we're surprised when we go out and try to gather crowds in, and expect them to respond to Jesus Christ. Why should they? We've not shown them that God loves them through us. When unemployment was their problem they didn't see us getting all worked up. When poverty was their problem they didn't see us getting all worked up. All these things have happened and the Christian Church has virtually said nothing. As though the gospel had nothing to say about that!

Well, go back to the Gospels and read the ministry of Jesus, and find out where He is all the time. He was very wise in not having headquarters. He had nowhere to be locked away. You would never find Him at the regular address, because there wasn't a regular address. So if you wanted to find Him you had to be where the poor were, because that's where He usually was. Or among the prostitutes (don't make that a soft word! It means what it says). Or among the betrayers of the nation, the tax-gatherers. It's not insignificant that the people who got the message first were shepherds. Shepherds because of their job couldn't be in the temple or synagogue; you can't say to sheep, 'Don't go away – I'll be back in an hour.' There's something very significant about the shepherds getting the message of the coming of the baby.

O my sisters and my brothers, that's what maturity is about!

C.H. Dodd many years ago distinguished between what he called *kērugma* and *didachē*. *Kērugma* is the gospel message at heart: Christ born, Christ living, Christ dying, Christ rising, Christ ascending, Christ coming again; the invitation to believe in Christ – that's *kērugma*. That's what the evangelist is concerned with all the time. The *didachē* is what the pastor does when the evangelist has moved on; *didachē* is what he has to teach the child of God, the babe.

Now, if the evangelist hasn't told the whole story, the pastor's going to be in great difficulty. But if the evangelist preaches the whole story, and the pastor tries to build his hearers up from somewhere else, he's still going to have great difficulty; because what the evangelist preaches is what we are then to apply to every part of national and international life.

And if we will not do it, we must not expect to win the world for Christ.

The quotation in verse 9 is from Isaiah 64:4, and probably from Isaiah 65:17. This word 'has prepared' is a very interesting one; Paul only uses it in this one place in his writings, and it doesn't occur very often in the New Testament. But it's a very significant word because it points us again to this idea we've kept coming across, that God's preparation of salvation can never be understood fully until you've gone through the whole range of it.

In other words, it comes back to that interesting word, 'eschatological'; it's about things not being finished yet, but which God has planned from the beginning. And how do we know about these things? Well, 'God has revealed it to us by his Spirit.' And it's interesting that this revelation comes 'to those who love him'.

In the first century, and perhaps even at Corinth, there were some people who placed a great deal of emphasis on 'knowledge'. They were the forbears of the heretics known as the Gnostics, which comes from a word which means 'to know'. So Paul doesn't say, 'What God has prepared for those who *know* him' – he says, 'for those who *love* him'. And to those who love Him, God reveals by His Spirit.

Can I amplify that? One of the dangers, as you think you are becoming more mature, is that you come to know more. But the danger is that as you know more, you can imperceptibly come to rely more on your knowledge than on your love. And I think that's why we find the great hymn of love in 1 Corinthians 13, where Paul says, 'If I know this, and can do this, that and the other, but cannot love – then I've missed the way.'

Senior Christian, senior Christian, with all your knowledge – how much do you love Him? Do you love Him more than you loved Him when you first came to know Him? As you know more, do you love more? Or does knowing more somehow dull your love?

Well, Paul's now introduced himself to a new topic. He's been talking about divine wisdom, now he's moved on to –

The work of the Spirit

Verse 10: 'The Spirit searches all things, even the deep things of God.' That word 'searches' doesn't mean looking for something when you don't know where it is. It means 'rummaging', it means getting out the photo album and saying, 'Do you remember that one? – Do you remember him? – Look at that hat!' You're not surprised at what you're finding; you know where it is, but you're rummaging.

That's this word. It says, 'The Spirit "rummages" among the things of God.' Isn't that nice? The Spirit doesn't say, 'Oh, where is that?' He 'rummages' among the things of God, and He reveals to us the deep things of God. That's why the mature are becoming mature, because they're discovering the deep things of God.

Now Paul uses a human analogy in verse 12. If you need a single verse that shows without any doubt that the Spirit is God, that's the one. That's the verse that says, beyond a shadow of doubt, that deity belongs to the Spirit. 'We have not received the spirit of the world' – that's the one he's been talking about, which the rulers of this age had so they couldn't understand the gospel – 'but the Spirit who is from God, that we may understand what God has freely given us.'

Understanding God's gift

Notice that there are two separate points in verse 12.

Firstly, *to receive what God gives is one thing, to understand it is another*. And I've learned a long time ago to distinguish between the validity of an experience and the accuracy of the description which the person having the experience gives to it. Sometimes you can hear somebody describing an experience, and you're sitting thinking, 'I can't accept that, I don't accept that; I don't believe that.' But don't draw the conclusion that the experience is invalid because the description isn't terribly accurate! There's a difference between having an experience and understanding it. That's the first point.

The second point is this: *we cannot understand the experience, unless God explains it to us*. And that's why the Bible has to be the inspired Word of God. Otherwise, how would we understand what God is doing in the world? Imagine yourself standing there when the creation took place, with all the breaking and the cracking and the rending and the burning and the thundering? Can you imagine yourself saying 'Ah! God is creating a universe of order'? I wouldn't – I'd be running for dear life! I'd be terrified.

Or imagine yourself standing at the foot of the cross saying, 'God is redeeming the world in Jesus.' I wouldn't be able to say that. Why? Because it isn't patently obvious what's going on.

That's what this letter is all about. Paul is saying, 'It isn't patently obvious; it's never patently obvious.' That's the point about spiritual wisdom. It isn't patently obvious. If it were, the Jews would have grasped it, the Gentiles would have grasped it, Pilate would have understood it, Caiaphas would have had it, and we'd all be in together. We only understand the spiritual things if God reveals the spiritual things.

That's why this book has to be reliable. If it isn't, where will we turn? You'd be at the mercy of people like me! That's a terrible fate to fall into!

A model for understanding

Verse 13: 'This is what we speak, not in words taught us by human wisdom but in words taught by the Spirit, expressing spiritual truths in spiritual words.' That's a very difficult verse in the Greek text because of grammatical problems with which I needn't trouble you. But I think this is the right translation: 'expressing spiritual truths in spiritual words'. Please notice the claim he's making for the teaching – 'not in words taught us by human wisdom'; that's the old lot he keeps on talking about, 'but in words taught by the Spirit'.

What a high doctrine of inspiration there is there: 'words taught by the Spirit'. That's why we attach so much importance to Scripture, isn't it? The man without the Spirit cannot, the man without the Spirit doesn't (or, better, *will* not) accept the things of the Spirit of God, for they are foolishness to him and he cannot understand them because they are spiritually discerned. Why don't some people grasp the gospel? They say it is because the gospel doesn't meet their needs. Paul says, that is not the explanation at all. Again, you see, the real reason is hidden. The explanation is that he or she is bringing the thoughts and wisdom of the world and applying them to the gospel. The reason the gospel isn't adequate for many people who hear it, is that they are not adequate to understand it.

That's what Jesus meant by the parable of the sower. That parable is not about the quality of the seed, it is a comment on the receptivity or non-receptivity of the soil. Therefore, some of us who work in difficult places, who are always in danger of being under criticism by those who think triumphally, should not take it personally. It's not to do with success, it's to do with faithfulness that we're in the ministry. If you're in a hard place, don't keep blaming yourself, don't keep looking longingly at the churches that are packed every week. Just ask yourself, 'Am I being faithful to the word? Am I being faithful to my Lord, am I loving these people and reaching out to them?' If you are, then that's the thing that matters. Leave the rest to God.

'The man without the Spirit does not accept the things that come from the Spirit of God' (verse 14). They are foolishness to him – it's the same word that is used in chapter 1 for the 'foolishness' of those who wouldn't have the gospel; he cannot understand these things, because they are 'spiritually discerned'. It means filtering through a lot of material to find what you want. It means the farmer going through the wheat, knowing how to get the chaff off. It means the coal miner knowing which coal is for selling and which is for the pit heap.

That's the word. And Paul says, the trouble with the worldly men and women is that they have no model, no system for sifting what happens to them in a way which enables them to understand what is going on.

A total world view

But notice what comes next. 'The spiritual person makes judgements about all things' – *panta* – why? Because, Paul is saying, once you have grasped the secret of the world, that Jesus Christ is the Word of creation, the clue of salvation, the centre point of consummation – once you have grasped that, then you are in a position to filter *everything* through that understanding, and to understand what God is trying to do with the world. You can say 'Through this filter, I can pass every piece of news, every political development, everything that any government does, anything which any family does, any development in any society whatsoever, and I will find that there is a comment from the gospel on that issue.'

I'm not sure you believe that. My guess is that all of us live more narrowly than that. But if God is God of all the world, if Jesus is who we have just said He is, what could be excluded? Nothing could be excluded!

The gospel is about the whole wide world. So don't tell me you're not interested in politics because you're a Christian, that you don't get involved in things in your society outside the Church because you're afraid of falling away; don't tell me you don't watch the news because it's so depressing, that at work you just get on with your job, and that you want nothing to do with trade unions or the way things are working out. I'm serious, my sisters and brothers.

The secret of the revival of the church in China, was that they cleared out all the missionaries (I speak as a former missionary!), got rid of most of the ministers, closed the churches, and threw the Christians in among the mass of the population – so what could they do? They simply lived the Christian life, and when someone was being treated badly, it was often the Christians who went and complained, even knowing the possible punishments. When people were ill, it was the Christians who went and looked after them, knowing that no-one was going to praise them for that, because illness was seen as weakness.

When the churches began to be opened again, people who had never been to church before turned to these folks. 'If you are the ones who go there, may we please come with you?' Those Christians didn't spend their time openly worshipping or having evangelistic campaigns. They couldn't. So what could they do? They said, 'Jesus Christ has something to say about every situation in life, so where I am is where He will be saying something.' So many people saw that the gospel applied so widely across life that there are now millions and millions of Christians in China, an unrecognisable number compared with what the missionaries managed to achieve.

Don't you believe that *this* is the wisdom?

The spiritual man makes judgement about all things, but 'he himself is not subject to any man's judgement'. That doesn't mean that we are above judgement. It doesn't mean that we can have tyrants in the Church who are so mature that nobody dare speak out about what they are doing. It means that outside the Christian Church, nobody has the model for judging us. How could they understand? Everything Jesus taught stands all human values on their head.

Think of the parable of the vineyard labourers: they worked for different lengths of time, but they all got paid the same. It's ludicrous, and it's very infuriating. It isn't fair at all!

But none of the parables *are* fair, because they're not about human justice, they're about the way God is establishing His kingdom. So how can people out in the world judge what we are about, and what we stand for? How can they make sense of our burying ourselves among the poor, and those who don't thank us? They haven't got the ability.

But by the grace of God, we, if we would patiently try to understand economics and politics, and sociology and psychology and union workings, whatever we are closest to, if we will try and understand what is going on, we will find that again and again, the gospel speaks its word.

Because – in the last sentence – 'we have the mind of Christ.'

My sisters and my brothers, most of us have made the mind of Christ so small, we should be ashamed of ourselves. For the mind of Christ thinks to the end of the universe. It takes everything that is happening right to the end of the universe. And we claim to have that mind, those of us who are going on to maturity.

1. This address is included on p.185 of the present volume.

4. Unity and Its Source
(1 Corinthians 3:1–23)

As we come to our final Bible study, I want to tell you, there is nothing like the fellowship we know here at Keswick. And I want to thank God for it, and to say how deeply I appreciate the fellowship of this platform.

The second thing I want to say is simply this: I hope that if you have found the Bible studies helpful, you will observe what underlies my method. It is the conviction that sound scholarship and deep devotion not only *can* go together – they *must* go together. There is no place for evangelical Christians to be afraid of scholarship. Please use all the powers you have intellectually, to learn as much as you can about what the word of God says. For, if persecution comes, we stand or fall on our knowledge of, and loyalty, to God's revelation in His Word.

Worldly Christians (3:1–4)

The word 'I' in these verses is very emphatic, because Paul is proceeding to a defence of himself. But 'brethren' – or 'brothers and sisters', as we have it translated today – is also emphatic. Paul is doing what I was talking about earlier; he is seeing them through the eyes of God in

Christ. In a moment, he's going to complain about them; he's going to tell them some things they're doing that are absolutely wrong. But they're still his brothers and sisters in Christ, because God has made them his brothers and sisters in Christ.

They may be way off the track, but he hasn't the right to say, 'You are no longer my brothers and sisters.' God in Christ still includes them. So whatever is coming, Paul still sees them as gathered into the Body of Christ, and therefore he sees the potential they have, once their being in Christ is worked out properly.

'I could not address you as spiritual but as worldly.' That's probably what they were saying about him, you see. They were probably complaining that when Paul came all he talked about was Jesus Christ and Him crucified. He didn't tell them about the great gifts of speaking with tongues, prophecy, knowledge and discernment, and all the things that were going to happen. So some of them at Corinth were saying, 'Well, I mean, is he really an apostle? All he gave us was the basic stuff.'

Paul says, 'Well, you're absolutely right, and now I'll tell you the reason – because babies aren't ready for beef, Yorkshire pudding and two veg! It's not that I didn't have it ready. I'd come from Athens, there was plenty I could have told you. But you were babies. It was you who limited what I did, not I. You were babies in Christ.'

Remember who he's talking to: this is the church that of all churches has most to boast about in spiritual gifts. They had teachers like Paul and Apollos. Maybe Peter too had visited. Maybe Cephas had been there. And yet they were still babies.

Feeding the babies
So let us be strong enough to learn the lessons. Don't expect too much of new converts. And I'm not thinking

only of what we say to them. That is not the strongest pressure. The strongest pressure on converts is what they find to be our unspoken expectations of them. That's the real pressure. They look to see what we do: how we dress, how we behave, how we address one another with our rather holy and pietistic way of speaking, the incredible performances in some of our services and the length of time they have to sit doing nothing on deliberately uncomfortable church seats.

And they watch our expressions as they tell us that they've been doing this or that – that they watch *Dallas* on TV, for instance – and our expressions communicate without words. 'Ah,' say the new converts, 'that wasn't the right thing to do.' Quite quickly they are on a track that actually has nothing to do with their being in Christ as babies; it has to do with some of our conceptions, and many of our misconceptions, about what it means to be mature.

So, my sisters and my brothers, if God gives you a baby to look after, don't expect it to be reading Greek tomorrow. It's a baby! And don't mistake exciting gifts for spiritual maturity, especially if you yourself have had some. There are some very mature Christians who don't have any exciting spiritual gifts at all. And there are some exciting people who have got all kinds of gifts, but you can tell they're babies from the way they use them.

And don't give a young convert a false impression of his or her strength. I was very interested to read that the footballer Glen Hoddle said just after he became a Christian 'Please don't parade me around. I may be a giant on the football field, but I'm a baby in the faith.' I'm putting those particular words into his mouth, but that was the thrust of what he said. Oh, these stars who get converted! They're immediately paraded all around the world as though just because they can sing or act or play football, somehow they'll be spiritual giants. But they're babies.

Going where people are

And do please begin where your baby is. If your baby cries, you don't go out into the garden with a bottle because it's nice out there. The bottle is destined for the baby's mouth, and you'll only find that where the baby is. You may wish the baby was somewhere else, but its crying shows that if you want to sleep you'd better get there with that bottle. 'I gave you milk,' Paul says, 'not solid food.' This is the person who will write Romans, about which Peter said, 'Brother Paul writes of things difficult to understand.' Amen, Peter, to that!

In Acts 17 Paul found himself debating in a debating society. The first half of his speech in Acts 17 is pure stoicism and epicureanism. His audience thought, 'It's just as well we asked him – he's a very good speaker, why haven't we heard of him before?' But, bit by bit, he starts talking about making up your mind – that's the last thing they want to do! – because God has established a day when He will judge. Now it's not so popular at all! How do you know He's going to judge? Well, He has raised somebody from the dead. They said, 'He's an idiot.'

The first half of the speech was given to them where they were. Do you see? Some people come to our worship and they're so amazed at all the strange things we do, they never hear the strangeness of the gospel. Jesus said, 'I have many things to say to you, but you cannot bear them now.' Again and again, the starting point in the teaching of the New Testament is not what the writer or the speaker chooses, but the condition and need of the readers or the hearers. The gospel preachers of the New Testament even selected from the gospel which parts of it they would preach, according to the need and condition of the hearers. They did not always preach the whole gospel, and in some of our churches they would not be welcomed!

'Indeed, you are still not ready.' Why? Verse 3: they're acting like mere human beings. One commentator says, 'It was reasonable then to expect them to be babes, but now they ought to be mature in Christ.' Is that your story, I wonder? Have you been lulled into believing that it doesn't really matter whether you understand or not, as long as you're at church? That your task is the lowly servant, that you don't really matter at all? That's heresy! Everyone in the pew matters. Everyone! All were equally died for, by God in Jesus Christ.

All of us who are ministers and pastors know that there are people in our congregations who have selective hearing. When they are asked for anything requiring some skill and ability, they just turn off – 'That couldn't mean me.'

Often, we preachers are to blame for that. Paul says, 'When one says "I follow Paul", and another says "I follow Apollos", are you not mere men?' The real tragedy is, they're leaving behind the mind of Christ, to try to feed themselves wholly on the mind of Paul or the mind of Apollos. I dread the possibility that everyone will go away from these Bible studies talking about how well Donald English does Bible studies. I'm being personal, but forgive me. You do me a great disservice if anything like that is said which distracts you in any way from being in Christ.

The tasks of the ministry

And now Paul comes in verses 5–10 to the tasks of the ministry. You might expect that the answer to the question at the beginning of the passage – 'What is Apollos, what is Paul?' – would be, 'Nothing'. But he doesn't say that. Preaching, as Philip Brooks says, is truth mediated through personality. So the opposite of making *too much* of your ministers or speakers or pastors, is to avoid making *nothing* of them, for that often betrays what you really think about the God who called them.

We are servants

We're servants, says Paul; that's the way to think of us.
The word means a table waiter. Paul doesn't say 'servants,
full stop', but 'your servants for Jesus's sake' (2 Cor. 4:5).
And then he tells us how they work together. He, Paul,
planted; Apollos watered, God made it grow. The meta-
phor has become that of agricultural labour.

God called the workers and gave them growth; so they
have nothing to boast of. So, says Paul, why gather round
people who have nothing to boast about? Why stand
around me? I've only got what I've been given. Wouldn't
it be better to talk to whoever's doing this stuff, like I do?
God will look after the reward anyway, he says: don't
please feel you are going to reward me for what I do. God
will give the reward.

We are God's fellow workers

Now, let me just pause. I believe something very significant is happening to the Christian Church today, and it's
this: I think we are coming to see that, in the mission of
the Church, evangelism, social caring, and the struggle for
justice all belong together. They belong together because
they're all in the Bible, and they are all in the Bible
because that's what God cares about. And therefore God
in His endless mission to the world is evangelising, and
caring, and seeking to establish justice, and He invites us
to join Him in this task. If we won't join, He will do it
without us. If we will join, the blessing is ours.

But it means that being part of the mission of God also
means being fellow workers with God, which means being
fellow workers with one another; which means that if I am
an evangelist at heart, I don't have to dismiss the social
carers and the strugglers for justice as somehow
unspiritual. If I'm a social carer I don't have to dismiss the
evangelist as someone who is long on words and short on

action. We each need each other in the one mission of God, and to be fellow workers with God means to be fellow workers with one another.

So you who are evangelists, start listening more to the social carers and the strugglers for justice. They can teach you a whole lot about the context of the people to whom you are preaching, what they are capable of and aren't capable of, and they'll teach you a whole lot about the chances of those people surviving in the faith. And you who are social carers and strugglers for justice, listen to the evangelists. They're telling you about the fact that you may change society, and you have to try to; but if you aren't changing hearts, then people aren't coming to know God.

We need to learn from one another. We are fellow workers in the field. If the focal point is God and His mission, then the Church is part of God's move to the world in mission. We are part of the focal point, and we are God's fellow workers; which means that questions about the shape and state of the Church, both in our evangelism, and in our own pastoral strategy, should not be answered in terms of our individual tradition and preferences. The dominant question is, 'Who is God, who is engaging in this mission?' And, 'Who are they, to whom we are going in mission?'

The other question I want to pose is this: What shape should a church be, which wishes best to reflect the nature and being of God in such a way that those outside can receive and respond to it? That's the question. And if I were a betting man I would bet that there hasn't been a single mission organised in the last ten years on that basis.

In a meeting which had lasted for an hour and a half, I heard somebody say, 'My people won't come to a mission in that town, because it's a bit up-market for them.' Somebody else said, 'Well, if it's held in your place, ours won't come, because it's down-market for them.' Another said, 'I hope it's not going to be too charismatic, my people can't stand this charismatic stuff.' Another said, 'If it's not charismatic, my folks won't come.'

It went on like that for an hour and a half – discussing a mission, would you believe! We hadn't talked about the people who were going to come. Nor had God had a word either. We were just making it comfortable for 'our' people. Can you hear any echo of that, I wonder, in your church?

Testing the foundations

No speaker in his right mind would choose to give a Bible study with a passage including verses 10–15! Let's start, however, with a tension which I think we can handle. Verse 10: 'By the grace God has given me, I laid a foundation as an expert builder.'

The average evangelical tends to reconcile the problem of how much of anything is God's doing, and how much is our's, by suggesting an 80/20 proportion – 'It's mostly God's doing, but I've got to do my bit.' When it starts shifting towards 75/25, we think we're slipping a bit into worldly attitudes.

But what is required is 100/100! That is, whatever you have to do, prepare it as an expert builder. If it's speaking, there's no grounds for saying: 'The Lord will provide.' The moments when the Lord will provide will be the moments when you couldn't provide. He'll give you the words then, never fear! But if you're going to speak next week, and you're saying, 'Now, the Lord will provide' – I confidently tell you, He won't, because you don't deserve to have His help.

I hope every pastor, preacher, and leader is listening to Paul. Careful preparation isn't likely to hinder God from blessing you. I think He could manage to bless you, even if you're thoroughly prepared! For you are offering into God's hands what the people are going to hear as God's word to you. So solve the problem of 'How much of Him, how much of me?' in the way suggested by that lovely hymn: 'All of me into His hands, none of self outside here.'

Everything I can do, given to Him; and He'll give everything He's got to it.

Each one builds, Paul says, verse 10b, but be careful how we build. I think that's a reference to the leaders in Corinth. Now, no-one can lay any foundation other than the one already laid, which is Jesus Christ. You now know much more about what that sentence means in view of the first two chapters we've been studying.

Tried by fire

Now comes the really difficult bit, the reference to gold and silver, costly stones, wood, hay and straw. They will be revealed with light, so that you will see what they are, and then they will be revealed with fire, because some will burn up, and some won't. Those whose work survives will receive a reward; those whose work is burnt will suffer loss. 'He himself will be saved, but only as one escaping through the flames.'

Let's hold on to what is certain. Even he who has built with the most combustible material is still going to be saved, though it will be a close thing. So Paul is not talking about salvation. What is he talking about?

He is using a kind of parable. He is saying, although we are saved by grace by faith, although it all depends on what God has done for us in Jesus, although all we can do is offer our faith into His hands – that does not mean we are free to be careless about the work we offer. Let me remind you, says Paul, if there's a fire, some things burn, and some things don't; and there *is* going to be a fire.

And on that day, the last day, when I stand and face my Lord, the question will not be, 'Did I think these four Bible studies were pure gold?' (I don't, incidentally!). The question will be, 'Will the fire of God's holiness burn them up?'

That's what Paul is saying. You won't lose your salvation by it; but oh, be as sure as you can, that when you get to glory the things you have done and the things you have offered were the very best that you were able to offer to Him. That's what he is saying. Paul is saying, the great day is going to be a great day. Just get gold ready for the great day.

Why? Because (verses 16–17) 'Don't you know? You yourselves are God's temple.' (The word used for temple is not the larger one, which included the sacred enclosure, it's *naos*, the place where the holy of holies was.) 'You' – and remember, most of these second persons are plural, not singular – 'you are the temple of God,' Paul says.

We tend, automatically, to individualise it. But the verbs are all plural. So it's not just a question of whether I'm trying to live holy, as God wants me to live. The question is my holiness is affected by yours, and your holiness is affected by mine. A much more serious question for me about holiness on the day of judgement is not whether I managed to be holy, but whether I helped you to be holy.

That's a real question. Some people manage to be holy at the expense of everybody else. But whoever destroys the temple will be destroyed. I think the Damascus Road may have been in Paul's mind here, when Paul was given that marvellous experience. Of course you remember; he said 'Who are you, Lord?' and received the reply, 'I am Jesus whom you are persecuting.'

If Paul hadn't been in such consternation, he might have said, 'But I'm not persecuting you, it's those people in Damascus called Christians I'm going to persecute.' To which Jesus would have replied, 'Precisely, Paul. You persecute them, you persecute Me.' So, my dear evangelical brothers and sisters (I include myself, I am addressing us all): let's be careful what we say about other branches of the Christian Church who don't exactly agree with us. You may find the Lord standing among them, there may be a question to answer on the last day about that.

Have a care, my sisters and my brothers. Of course there will be times when we have to tell one another that we're wrong. I'm talking about that. I'm talking about the ease with which we dismiss whole areas of the Christian Church with a whole variety of adjectives which I don't need to spend time on. Maybe the Lord is in the midst of all of that. So, be careful.

Conclusion (3:18–23)

Now, we are starting to pull it all together. Don't, Paul says, think worldly-wise ways. What does he mean? He means, don't think in ways which actually show that you really believe that human beings are at the centre of the universe.

We preachers have some awful temptations to assume that our sermons will go well because of what we ourselves contribute. It's worldly! Whether a sermon goes well or not depends on how God blessed those who heard. If you all come up to me afterwards and say, 'Wonderful, marvellous,' that doesn't demonstrate anything. It doesn't say that the work of the Kingdom has been put forward. It might say that I have entertained you tolerably for nearly an hour a day. That's worldliness. But the test on the last day will be: 'Will these four Bible studies still be there

when the fire is over?' And I've no way of knowing that.
Have you?

The foolish world

Worldliness is a great temptation. I have to say, I've seen
in the Church little men and little women behaving like
dictators, because in the church they had spiritual gifts,
and outside the church they don't even count for anything.
Beware of the worldliness that comes along with authority
and ability!

So, in 19–20, Paul is most dismissive about the wisdom
of the world: 'foolishness in God's sight'. He's still talking,
remember, about salvation, so he quotes from Job 5:13
and Psalm 94:11. I wonder whether the reference to craftiness means there was a certain amount of craftiness in
Corinth. I wonder whether those who didn't like him were
manoeuvring to try to get him never invited again.

I wonder whether you've noticed, in the world at large,
that the people who seem to be in control of things are
often the people who fall furthest; the people who seem to
be able to control everything, suddenly come such a crop-
per. I think it may be true in the Christian life. It may be a
law actually built into the universe that whoever thinks
that he or she has got it all under control, and works
desperately to achieve that, will find things are never
capable of being totally controlled; something from
nowhere pops up and destroys it all.

There are well-known people who seem to have it all
made, and then suddenly, inexplicably, down they go. I
think it's because we're not intended to have everything
under control. Every day's a day of new receiving from
God of life; every day we're saying, 'Lord, if you do not
sustain then I am lost.'

When I went up to the University of Leicester, after a
year they asked me to look after the bookstall. I had to

stand there in the main hallway once a week and be
prepared to speak to non-Christians who wanted to ask
questions. Oh, the nervousness, the afraidness, the risking
of myself, every Tuesday lunchtime! But I think I learned
more in those Tuesdays than I'd learned in most other
situations. Every day I had to say, 'Lord, if you don't keep
me I really am done for. And then what will happen to
your kingdom?' Well, I've learned that I needn't have
worried too much about the second half of that question . . .

Charles Wesley, towards the end of the Evangelical
Revival, wrote to a friend in Ireland: 'The difference
between myself and John was that my fear was first for the
Church and then for the Methodists; his concern was first
the Methodists and then the Church' (by which he means
Church of England). Then he wrote, 'Our differences
were in relation to temperament; mine all fear and his all
hope.' The Methodists didn't know from day to day what
was going to happen next. But every day John Wesley
believed that God would keep him.

The venturing Church
Therefore the call is to us to launch out into the deep. The
'Keep Sunday Special' campaign showed what the Christian Church in England can do if it really sets its mind to
it. But you see, we chose something of our own, didn't
we? It's a marvellous cause, I'm still fully committed to it.
But ought we not to be risking ourselves a bit more – in
areas where perhaps we're not as aware at the moment as
we might be?

I'm certainly not pleading for 'moral majority', which is
narrow platform politics. It chooses half a dozen things
that the Christians really feel strongly about, and meas-
ures all politicians by how they stand on those issues.
That's not what I'm talking about. I'm talking about being

death-and-resurrection people who risk themselves in
seeking to work for the kingdom of God all over the
world, knowing that every day's a risk, that every day we
might fall into some situation where we haven't got an
answer, that every day we risk our very lives for His sake.

That's what death-and-resurrection people do. Why is
the church in China now growing? Why is what's happening in Russia happening? Because people have risked
themselves. Why is the church growing in Korea? People
talk about the prayer meetings there – that's absolutely
right. Did you know that Korea is the most invaded country in the world? I think it's been invaded over 900 times.
And every time the invaders have come, the Christians
and the missionaries from outside stood with the native
Koreans. They put massive investment into education,
which has enabled the Korean people to reach the point
where they are amongst the most profound people in the
world. And they started lending societies, to help peasant
Koreans begin to grow. That's why the gospel spreads in
Korea; not just for the praying. But because the Korean
missionaries had wide vision and stood by the people in
every part of their experience.

All things are yours

Isn't that what we should be doing? Because, you see,
Paul says – and here I must finish – 'all things are yours.'
Why fiddle around chasing after Apollos and Paul, when
everything is yours? Everything is yours – forgiveness,
fellowship in the church, a code for understanding the
world. What God did in Jesus has given us the code by
which to understand what the whole of the world's about;
life with all its meaning, death as destroyed by the resurrection, the present because you're being sanctified, the
future because we're moving on to the eschaton; it's all

ours my sister and brother, this whole wide world belongs to us. Because God's given into our hands not just the world as we see it, but the knowledge which enables us to understand it.

We know that you don't get happiness by chasing it, but by becoming holy. We know that you gain your life by giving it away. We know that the strongest power in the world is love, so we don't have to keep hitting people back. We know that every moment of time has eternity behind it. We know all that, don't we? Then the world is ours!

And the politicians, and the economists, and the sociologists and all these other people – they need to know it. They think that by their methods they can achieve it. But we possess it all. It's all ours. And yet we hide away in our little tabernacles having another this or another that, planning next year's anniversary – but the world is ours!

I finish with a testimony. I came to Keswick as a student who was supposed to be the leader of the Christian Union. I was totally unequipped for the job, and, to make it worse, they were into the 'second blessing'. And I didn't even know what the first blessing was!

So I came here looking for the 'second blessing'. I was desperate. I came to every meeting, desperately wanting to know about the 'second blessing'. And in one day I talked to three different people: Major Bill Batt, who used to run the IVF camp; one of our African brothers; and a Christian woman from my own university. None of them knew the others or knew about the other conversations. But they all said, 'It's all in Jesus.'

I went back from the last conversation to my tent in the IVF camp. Everybody else was asleep in the tent; it was so late. And I knelt beside my camp bed, and I said, 'Lord, I'm at my wits' end. I don't understand the theories of sanctification, but I do know that whatever You want from me, I give it now. I give everything now.' And I went to sleep.

The next day, two of us hitch-hiked home. We came to a road cafe, and there was a tramp there cursing and swearing. And I felt from within me this Christ to whom the night before I had given my life, say, 'Go to him.' I thought, 'Hmmmmm!' But I went over and sat down, and he looked up and started swearing and cursing, and I said, 'Do you know Jesus Christ loves you?' And he burst into tears. There and then in that place, the Christ to whom I had given my life the night before used me to show the way of salvation to this man.

Now that is what it's all about. Not Paul, not Apollos, not this speaker; not this denomination, not that denomination; it's about Christ – the wisdom of God and the righteousness of God. Christ crucified, Lord of all. And in Him you have everything, because you are in Christ, and Christ is in God, and that's how it's going to be for all eternity; thank God!

LIVING FAITH FOR PRACTICAL PEOPLE

by Rev. Stuart Briscoe

1. Trials, Temptations and Things To Do (James 1:1–27)

[This address was given in St John's Church, Keswick, following the wrecking of the Convention tent by gales.]

I want to commend everybody on their adaptability and good humour. If you can't be adaptable in England you certainly cannot possibly survive! We've had to make some changes, of course. We were going to video this, and I'm deeply disappointed that it isn't going to happen now, because I put on a jacket and tie![1]

Let's turn to the Epistle of James, and the first two verses. The Epistle of James has had a somewhat chequered history, as far as acceptability in the Church of Jesus Christ is concerned; and even as recently as dear old Martin Luther, there were some reservations as to whether it belonged in the canon of Scripture at all. He, you may remember, said in his Preface to the New Testament: 'This is an epistle full of straw, because it contains nothing evangelical. I do not hold it to be of apostolic authorship.' (Martin Luther did also say 'If a woman dies in childbirth it matters not; she's made for it.' So there were some things on which he wasn't altogether correct!)

The reason that he was so upset about James was that he thought James was contradicting his beloved Paul, particularly the epistles to the Galatians and the Romans where the emphasis of course is on justification by grace through faith. Luther thought that James was teaching that a man is justified by works. That was one reason why he felt it was full of straw and there was nothing evangelical in it.

Another reason was that the Lord Jesus is only mentioned twice in the whole of the epistle, and so Luther felt that it just didn't match up to the general tone of Scripture. As we shall see, he was misreading the epistle.

Notice that James goes straight into his subject. The apostle Paul was rather given to long introductions. James, we'll find, is a very practical down-to-earth sort of man, and he just decides to get straight down to it. Paul would sometimes require a chapter, or a chapter-and-a-half, to say what James says in that brief verse 1.

Then he gets straight into his subject: 'Consider it pure joy, my brothers, when you face trials of many kinds.' In this first chapter we'll talk first about trials, then about temptations, and then we'll gather up the things that remain and simply call them 'things to do'.

Trials (1:1–12)

Now the key word here is 'trials' – the Greek word is *peirasmois*. It is a very important word; we're going to come across it many, many times in this epistle.

Trials are inevitable

The first thing to notice about trials is that they are *inevitable*. James does not say, 'Consider it pure joy, my brothers, *if* you face trials.' There is absolutely no question about it, the Christian *will* face trials. The Lord Jesus made this very clear speaking to His disciples. He said, 'In the world you will have trouble.'

It's very frank of Him, and of course very different from much preaching that we hear today. The impression sometimes given today by His disciples is that when you come to Jesus, everything will suddenly be wonderful; there'll be blue skies and bright sunshine and everything will be just perfect. But in fact the Lord Jesus said just the opposite. And so it is no surprise to us to discover that trials are inevitable.

This is understandable from James's own point of view, for

Trials are inevitable from James's personal experience

Notice three things here that show us that James would understand the inevitability of trials from his own experience.

1. *He had a brother who had suffered deeply*. You know who his brother was, don't you, or, more accurately, his half-brother?

Now some people will debate this, but I believe that the James of this epistle is the half-brother of our Lord Jesus Christ, and that he had seen the intense suffering that Jesus had gone through.

We know that the Lord Jesus had half-brothers and sisters. He certainly had four half-brothers that we know of: James, in all probability the eldest; Jude, you remember – the writer of the other epistle – another of them; and we also know that while there were three or four James's in the New Testament, there's a very good case to be made for this James being the one who was related to the Lord Jesus.

It's interesting to notice that this particular James was not always a follower of the Lord Jesus. In fact, during Jesus' lifetime, James and his other brothers were highly critical of Him, and in fact we're told quite categorically in one place that His brothers did not believe in Him.

But then a very dramatic thing happened; Jesus rose from the dead, and afterwards made some very carefully selected post-resurrection appearances. And 1 Corinthians 15:7 tells us that one of those was to His half-brother James.

So when we see James – brought up in the same home as his half-brother Jesus, critical, unbelieving, sceptical, antagonistic towards his half-brother for thirty-three years – confronted with the risen Lord, and then calling him at the beginning of his epistle 'the Lord Jesus Christ', we are seeing one of the most dramatic conversions of all times.

But, back to my point, which is that James understands the inevitability of trials, because he watched his half-brother at close quarters, and came to the conviction that his half-brother was none other than the Lord Jesus Christ. And Jesus suffered intensely.

2. *He knows of the twelve tribes who were scattered among the nations.* This could be interpreted in different ways. He could, as a Jew writing mainly to Jews, have been thinking primarily of Jewish history. If that was so, no doubt he was thinking of the captivity under the Assyrians, the later captivity under the Babylonians, and the later dispersion under the Romans. He probably recognised that the Jews had been scattered from their homeland all over the world.

But it is also quite possible that he was thinking of another kind of dispersion.

After the post-resurrection appearances, James became a very significant member-leader of the church in Jerusalem. You will also remember that Stephen was martyred in Jerusalem, and afterwards terrible persecution was poured out on the church there. The Christians fled, and it was said that wherever they went they preached the

Lord Jesus, and the hand of the Lord was with them, and a great number believed and turned to the Lord.

One of the places they went to was Antioch of Syria, and a church was born there. The Jewish leaders sent Barnabas from Jerusalem to check on it, and he was thrilled with what he saw. He decided to find Saul of Tarsus, and brought him back to teach in Antioch, and you remember that Saul and Barnabas taught there until one day in a worship service the Spirit of God somehow identified Saul and Barnabas as the two people who were to be sent out of that church, and they went off on their missionary journeys.

So James may possibly be thinking of the scattered Church, for he fully recognises that down through the history of the Jewish people there have been all kinds of persecution. They had been subjected to trials, they had been subjected to problems; and he also knows that in the history of this fledgling church that they had been subjected to trials, they had been subjected to difficulties, and it is probably to them that he is writing.

We cannot say conclusively whether he is writing primarily to Jewish people who are not believers, or whether he is writing to Jewish Christians who fled from Jerusalem and were dispersed. But as far as our point is concerned, he knows that trials are inevitable. From his own experience, he's seen his own brother suffer terribly, and he has seen the scattering of his brothers and sisters in Christ and in the Jewish people.

3. *He has now become a servant.* Verse 1: 'James, a servant of God, and of the Lord Jesus Christ.' We're familiar with this word 'servant'; it is the word *doulos*. It means someone who belongs, who gives of himself without any concern for his own unique concerns and well-beings; it means someone who makes himself or herself available to another person.

And if you're going to be a servant, to belong to another, to recognise that you do not have rights to your own life, it's going to be a very testing experience; because it militates against everything that is inherently human.

It's true that he has become the pillar of the church at Jerusalem, as Paul calls him in Galatians 2:9; it's true that when they had the great Council at Jerusalem, recorded for us in Acts 15, James was clearly its chairman. But nevertheless James still knows what it is to be a *doulos*, a servant – and it's a testing role. So he has no difficulty at all in telling us that trials are inevitable, from his personal experience.

I think if we can see James in this light, it will help us to understand this epistle better.

I remember a few years ago talking to Josef Ton, the pastor from Rumania. He is exiled now and lives in the United States. He was talking about the difference between the church in the United States and the church in Rumania.

'Let me illustrate it to you like this,' he said. 'Whenever I go into churches in America where the pastor is teaching the book of Revelation, it almost seems as if his primary concern is to assure the American church that it will not go through the tribulation. But the church in Rumania has a totally different approach. There, they realise that the book of Revelation was written by John, the Bishop of Ephesus, the pastor. And they recognise that he was in exile, and they recognise that the Ephesians were having a hard time.'

So as far as the Rumanian church is concerned, they see the book of Revelation as a letter to a persecuted church, by an exiled pastor who himself is going through times of deep testing, writing to people who are going through times of deep testing together, and it is written so that they can stand firm.

I suggest to you that James in exactly the same way is writing, as somebody who has a personal knowledge of testing, to the scattered believers about what testing means.

Trials are inevitable from normal Christian experience

In verses 3 and 4, James goes on to show that trials are inevitable, not just from his own experience, but from normal Christian experience. He shows us that *peirasmois*, 'testings', are an inevitable part of the Christian experience because they have a determined, designed end. There is purpose to them.

The word he uses is the word that describes somebody 'falling into a testing', into a problem, into a trial. In the Philippines recently I saw an open manhole, and was told that it was extremely dangerous during the rain and floods – sometimes people forgot it was there under the water and fell into it. That's the word that James uses to describe how testing times will come: you suddenly fall into them.

Two other uses of this word will, I think, be helpful illustrations. A certain man going down from Jerusalem to Jericho 'fell among thieves' – the same word.

You remember also that once Paul and some of his friends and some who were not particularly friends were sailing in a ship. He had warned them not to do it. They ran into a terrible storm and the ship was falling apart – and then they 'hit a sandbank'. It's exactly the same word.

There's the picture. You either fall into a flooded manhole, or you fall among thieves on the way from Jerusalem to Jericho, or you hit a sandbank and, before you know, you're in over your head. That is the image that James uses to describe the way these testing times will come.

But notice also that he speaks of different kinds of testings. The word that he uses to describe these different kinds of testings, *poikilois*, means literally 'many-coloured', 'variegated'. James is telling us that the trials – the testings that we fall into – come suddenly; we fall into them – and in addition to that, they come in many varied shades or colours.

Jay Adams puts it this way, with a fine touch of imagination in creativity: 'Our testings can come in the fiery reds of affliction, the icy blues of sorrow, the murky browns of failure, the sickly yellows of illness and disease'.

As we think of the testing times that we have been subject to, we recognise that they come in many varied forms. However, always remember that Peter, writing on a similar subject, also points out to us (in 1 Peter 4:10) that the grace of God comes in variegated forms, using the same word *poikilois*. Whatever the situation might be, the grace of God is adequate for it.

Some of the testings that people fall into are really rather predictable. You watch what they're doing, you try to encourage them but you try to warn them: 'Look, if you do this you're going to be in all kinds of trouble.'

I think of some people who have come to talk to us about their marriages. They talk about the terrible problems that they have, and then they say brave things like, 'Well, I suppose it's the cross I have to bear.' But you sometimes wonder whether that is the case, because the marriage problems that they have were totally predictable.

One woman married three times, against all our advice (remarriage isn't wrong for everybody, but for this woman we felt it was a tragic mistake). And the testings – in her case, a long chapter of many and varied testings – were predictable.

But for others, the testings they fall into are utterly inexplicable. I think of another woman in our church: a beautiful young widow, the mother of three or four children. Her husband died completely unexpectedly. She

was distraught, and the whole church was distraught with
this. A year or two later she met another wonderful young
man; they married, and the whole church rejoiced with
them. They had a baby. And one day the baby was found
dead in his crib. The whole church wept with them. It was
utterly inexplicable.

Sometimes these testings are totally predictable; sometimes they're utterly inexplicable. But, James tells us, they
are inevitable. You suddenly fall into them. Before you
realise what's happened, they will come in many varied
forms.

In verse 9, James gives us two illustrations of the different
ways that testings can come to different types of people.

The testings of the poor man are totally different from
those of the rich man. The poor man feels so oppressed,
so neglected, that if he's not careful he can become very,
very bitter, cynical, envious. But he has to recognise that
these testings have a desired end; and he is going to
experience the desired end (which we'll get to in a
moment or two) when, instead of dwelling on the testings
that come as a result of his poverty, he begins to take
pride in his high position. He may be nothing much in the
social economy of his day, but he's a child of the King.
And as a child of the King he is rich beyond his wildest
dreams. Therefore he will certainly have variegated, col-
oured testings as a poor man. But he can come out rich as
a result.

The testings of the rich man are quite different. We
have a saying in America, that some self-made men worship their creator! I think that expression, 'self-made
man', must be one of the most insulting expressions we
can ever use in front of God. The apostle Paul puts it in
perspective in 1 Corinthians 4:7 with the great rhetorical
question: 'What do you have, O Man, that you have not
received?' So much for the self-made man!

But the testing of the rich man, the self-made man, is that he has been brought to the position of believing that money will buy anything, and that if he throws it around often enough, far enough, in the right direction, he can cope with everything; and he needs to recognise that that is a test. If he doesn't learn to humble himself before God, he's heading for a fall. The rich man like the rest is just like a flower that flourishes – he might be a big flower, he might be a bright flower, he might have a tremendous impact on his society, but it's only a matter of time until he will wither and die.

So the testings of the poor man and the testings of the rich man are just the opposite. Yet given the appropriate response, both can produce things of value. So James introduces us to the subject of testings by pointing out to us that testings – trials – are inevitable.

Trials are valuable

Now, let's go back to verse 2. James doesn't say, 'Now when you have trials just cheer up folks, you know it could be worse.' He says 'Consider it pure joy, because' – and notice his reasons – 'you know that the testing of your faith develops perseverance. Perseverance must finish its work so that you may be mature and complete, not lacking anything.' In other words, trials are valuable for two reasons.

Faith's centre and calibre must be tested by fire

Faith must always be put through the fire to test its centre and to try its calibre. Of course everybody has faith. We all instinctively operate on the basis of trust. We are full of this stuff called 'faith'. The big question is – faith in what?

'Now,' says John, 'testings will come in order that your faith might be tested.' You see, you can have tremendous

faith in your own physical fitness until you get sick. And
you can have tremendous faith in your doctor until he tells
you he's sorry he can't diagnose your problem. The whole
point is that our faith should be centred in the God who is
worthy of our faith; and sometimes it takes testings – trials
– to prove to us that the centre of our faith is not where it
should be.

The calibre of our faith needs testing too, because so
often our faith has so many inadequate and inappropriate
accretions. They need to be burned off; they need to be
taken away. It's imperative that we go through the trials in
order that the core and the calibre and the centre of our
faith might be revealed.

Perseverance must be produced by fire

But there's another reason, and that is so that the testing
might produce perseverance: *hupomonē*. That does not
mean a passive, fatalistic resignation to the inevitable. It is
an active, positive word. What James is really saying is
that these testing times are tremendously valuable, not
only because they will test the core, and the centre, and
the calibre of our faith; but also because these testings,
when responded to appropriately, will begin to produce in
us a rugged, active, positive, steadfastness. The best way I
can summarise it in contemporary English is to use that
well-known saying, 'When the going gets tough, the tough
get going.'

There is a calibre of spiritual toughness that is engen-
dered through the trials and the testings. And that's the
first reason that trials are valuable.

But the second reason is that when this toughness and
spiritual perseverance has been produced, it becomes pro-
ductive in and of itself. James proceeds to explain what is
produced: 'Perseverance must finish its work, so that you
may be mature, complete, not lacking anything' (verse 4).

There are three words there: 'Mature', 'complete' and 'not lacking anything'. The Christian believer who comes under testing times has produced within himself or herself a spiritual toughness. And that toughness keeps them aggressively, actively pressing on, 'keeping on keeping on'; and as they keep on keeping on, so they are perfected – they are matured.

James uses the word *teleios* for 'mature'. It means, to be fitted for the end in view. In other words, God has something in mind for you, and He knows that He is going to equip you for that particular task as you respond appropriately to testing times and have this quality of perseverance produced in you. And as you continue to persevere, the result will be that slowly but surely, you'll be more and more fitted for the end He had in mind.

The other word is 'complete'. The word means to be what in cricket parlance we would call an 'all-rounder'. Let me give you another analogy. You may have seen body-builders on television. If you listen to the commentators, they will be saying, for example, that a contestant has highly-developed pectorals, but their calves are underdeveloped. And if that contestant is ever going to make it in the big time, he is going to have to concentrate less on his pectorals and work on his calves.

'Now then,' says James, 'the testing times will come, and as you respond appropriately to them, you will be more and more fitted for the end in view and there won't be any glaring weak spots. You'll become an all-rounder.'

And finally he states negatively what he has just stated positively: 'You will be complete, not lacking anything.'

So James tells us that trials are inevitable and trials are valuable.

Trials are manageable
Now we go back to verse 2. How do we manage these trials? Let me suggest to you three specific things:

1. *Carefully consider*. We need to carefully consider what is going on. Notice the word with which verse 2 begins – 'consider'. It means 'count', or 'direct your thinking'. The way you think about a situation will to a very large extent determine how you respond to it. And so it is imperative that we get our thinking straight.

We've been trying to think through this business of *peirasmois*, how trials are inevitable but how they're also valuable. We have got to think this through.

2. *Continually confess*. But not only are we to carefully consider; we are to continually confess certain things.

What sort of things are we to confess if we are to manage our trials properly? Well, look at verses 5–8.

We have to confess a lack of wisdom. These trials are coming, and we have to say to God, 'God, I lack wisdom!'

Let's be careful that we understand what we mean by wisdom. Wisdom is knowing what is right, and knowing how to do what is right. There's a difference between knowledge and wisdom. We have many doctors in our church back home. One of them, a research gynaecologist, once said to me, 'Stuart, the main problem that we have today in the United States is that our technology is ahead of our morality.' And she said, 'Your job is to keep our feet to the fire morally. We'll handle the technology, but don't ever let us off the hook! Keep our feet to the fire.'

Wisdom is different from knowledge. Knowledge is simply a data bank. Wisdom is knowing what in the world to do with it. And so when we think in terms of lacking wisdom under trials and testings, what we're really saying is, 'What is the right thing to do in response to this situation? And how do I do it? And God, I have to freely confess, I don't right now know what is the right thing to do and I don't know how to do it.'

We continually confess this. This is how we manage testings. We get our minds right, thinking this thing through, then we confess, we lack wisdom.

We have to confess we need help. 'If any of you lacks wisdom, ask . . .' Ask! Ask! Don't just go out there and say, 'Well, we've just got to grit our teeth and roll up our sleeves and make the best of it. Life is harsh . . .' No. You confess you lack wisdom and you confess you need help.

We confess that we are totally dependent. We ask in faith. We're totally dependant on God to be the source of wisdom and the source of power to cope with the testing in order that the desired end might be achieved – not 'doubting' and not 'double-minded'.

But then notice, *we also confess that we are fully expectant that God will do something*. Who is this God of whom we ask? Verse 5: 'He gives generously to all without finding fault, and if we ask for wisdom it will be given.'

He's a giving God. Sometimes we think God gives grudgingly. Not at all!

So trials are manageable when we carefully consider, when we continually confess and, thirdly, when we

3. *Cheerfully celebrate*. Cheerfully celebrate testings? Yes! 'Consider it pure joy!' – we're back in verse 2. Celebrate! Not celebrate the *testings*? – 'Oh good! Here I am again this morning, God, and I feel rotten! Hal-le-lu-jah!'?

That's not what He has in mind. 'Here I am this morning, dear Lord; I feel absolutely rotten. I've got a rainbow of varied many-coloured testings. But I'm glad that You're a giving, and a generous and a gracious God, and I know that You have an end in view, and I'm glad that it gives me a chance to identify the centre and the core and the calibre of my faith, and I believe that there's a high probability that if I respond appropriately to the wisdom

You give me, I'm going to come out of this thing tested
and tried like gold.'

Temptations (1:12–18)

Now we move on. Notice now in verse 13 the word
'tempted' appears. The thing that's rather confusing for us
is that the word that we've already been introduced to,
peirasmois, is sometimes translated 'trial' and sometimes
'temptation'. It's the same word. So if we're to approach
temptations properly, we need two things. We need first
of all a proper perspective on trial and then, secondly, we
need a proper perception of temptation. So first of all,
getting the right perspective on temptation is a matter of
meaning.

Look at it this way: when a testing comes your way, that
testing gives you one of two choices; either the opportunity to do right, or the opportunity to go wrong. If you
do right, it proved to be a testing. If you do wrong, that
same set of circumstances proved to be a temptation.
And, in exactly the same way, circumstances responded to
one way resolve themselves into the maturity that comes
from testing, but when not responded to appropriately can
produce all kinds of things.

What kind of things? James tells us quite frankly that
what can be produced, as a result of these testings to
which we have not responded to properly, are all kinds of
most inappropriate things.

Notice first of all that when we get a proper perception
of temptation, we do so *when we reject some theories, and
when we respect some truths*.

Let me suggest one or two theories about temptation
that we should reject. One is, 'God is tempting me. It's
God's fault.' Another is, 'The devil made me do it.'

There's a black comedian in America called Flip
Wilson, who portrays a woman character as a woman

whose favourite expression was, 'The devil made me do it!' That is Flip Wilson theology. It is an inappropriate response to testing.

'The woman You gave me' is another quite common response. Or 'My father ate sour grapes and unfortunately my teeth have been set on edge!' That was an old one in the Old Testament, and they were told they shouldn't use it any more.

We must reject certain theories about why we behave the way we do.

And we must respect certain truths about temptation. You will find them in verses 14 and 15. The first truth is this: there is within each one of us a whole catalogue of things called 'desires'. The word James uses is *epithumias*, sometimes translated in the old Bible versions as 'lusts', which gives us the idea that *epithumias* is always a bad thing.

But it is not necessarily so. There are desires within us that are perfectly legitimate. God has placed sexual desires in us for the propagation of the human race. He has placed desires for food within us in order that we might have the nourishment to carry on to His glory. So a desire can be perfectly legitimate, but it can be twisted and warped and abused.

Now, if that twisting of a *legitimate* desire takes place deep down within me, because of my fallenness, then it is possible that if I am exposed to external testing and respond out of a *warped* desire, I will be dragged down. And that's what James says here: 'Each one is tempted by him when by his own evil desire, he is dragged away and enticed.'

The word 'dragged away' means to be hooked like a fish. A situation comes along, and it's not my fault; there is a desire within me that at first was legitimate; but now it's got warped and twisted and I've hung around long

enough so that the hook is set in my mouth. Before I
realised what had happened I was being dragged away.
And in the end, I'm landed, slopping, utterly defeated.

'Now,' James says, 'the result of this is that that situation' – and here we change the analogy from a fish on a
hook to the process of fertilisation and conception – 'this
situation that was a testing to prove me, has turned into a
temptation that has produced sin and death.' We have to
respect the truth of this. That's how temptation works.

We also need to respect the truth about God. James
talks about God's *character*. To coin a word, 'He is not
temptable.' He is utterly holy. There is nothing in Him
that would respond to an external event in such a way that
it would produce sin. Not only is He not temptable, He
does not tempt; He permits, He ordains, He allows, He
uses tempting, but never with a view to our sinning –
always with a view to our maturing. He never solicits us to
evil, He would always encourage us to good.

Now we need to get the truth right about God – His
character and His *changelessness*. The sun, moon and
stars go on shining, and He is the Father of those lights.
He goes on shining graciously, generously, givingly
towards us, unchanging, pure and holy in His character,
making available to us all that we need, in order that we
might respond as we ought. (Some commentators think
that there might be a sort of oblique reference to astrology
at this point; that the Father of lights is the one who in the
very lights that he governs demonstrates His
unchangeableness, and it is a nonsense to suggest that our
fate is in the stars.)

We begin to handle temptation aright as we respond to
the truth about God, His character, His changelessness,
and His *choice*, for James tells us that He chose; 'He chose
to give us birth' – verse 18 – 'through the word of truth,
that we might be a kind of first-fruits of all that he
created.'

He took a divine initiative, in marked contrast to the idea of testings; finding within us a desire that was warped and one impregnating and conceiving and bringing forth sin. In marked contrast to that, God chose to impregnate us by His Spirit, and generate within us a response that would result in the new birth. And the whole point of this new birth is that we might grow and mature, and in so doing become a kind of firstfruits to God, the beginning of the harvest, separated, holy, unto God.

That's what we're supposed to be as testing times come, as we respond to them appropriately, as we resist falling into temptation and recognise that God has freely chosen to impregnate us by His Spirit so that we might be born again through the ministry of the Word of God. As new creations under testing we mature and we become holy unto the Lord, as firstfruits. That's how we're supposed to handle temptation.

Things to do

Thirdly, things to do. I'm simply going to give you a list. Remember, they have as their objective the bringing about of the righteous life that God desires (verse 20). That's the key.

1. We've got to do something about anger.

2. We've got to do something about filthiness.

(The word 'filthy' here is the word translated 'shabby' in 2:2. We've got to do something about the shabby, filthy things we do.)

3. We've got to do something about the Word of God.

4. We've got to do something about our tongues.

5. We've got to do something about the needy people around us.

And if we handle all those things in the power of the Spirit, drawing on the generous, gracious, ungrudging provision of our God, then when we go through trials they will not degenerate into temptations, and we will become increasingly mature: the first-fruits – set apart for God.

1. This study was repeated later in the week, and a video recording made then.

2. Favouritism, Faith and Tongues of Fire
(James 2:1–3:12)

Favouritism

In chapter 2 verse 1, James, the ever practical one, the one who is concerned that faith should demonstrate itself in action, addresses a very pertinent subject: favouritism. He is rather blunt and straightforward.

A powerful exhortation
It is a powerful exhortation. It is addressed to brothers, and it is addressed to believers. While James is very blunt and very straightforward, he does soften what he has to say with the word 'brothers' (this of course is the modern translation of the old word 'brethren', and it includes 'sisters' as well).

There's a family aspect to this; he isn't just giving us a blunt command, he is addressing those who because they have been born of the same Spirit, born through the same engrafted word, are members of the same family.

But notice also that this exhortation is addressed to believers; literally, 'those who hold the faith'. Yesterday we were talking about our faith being tested, and tried. Here's one of the ways in which those whose faith is being

tested can evaluate what's coming through the testing. Do
they show favouritism, or not?

This is a very practical application of what James introduced in 1:27 of the previous chapter: 'Religion that God
our Father accepts as pure and faultless is this: to look
after orphans and widows in their distress . . .' In other
words, he is eager to remind the brothers and the
believers in our Lord Jesus Christ that that religion of
theirs is going to be characterised by a marked concern for
the under-privileged. His concern is that practical spiritual
experience should manifest itself in a concern for them,
whether orphans or widows or impoverished.

Notice, also, that this exhortation is related to the Lord
Jesus Christ. The NIV translates it as 'our glorious Lord
Jesus Christ'. The Greek here is a little difficult to translate. It means literally 'the Lord Jesus Christ of the glory',
and various people have tried to interpret this in different
ways. Let me suggest to you that they all seem to be
pointing to the fact that our Lord Jesus Christ is our glory,
He is our standard, He is our star, He is the one we look
to, He is our model. And so if we are to understand why
we should not show favouritism, it is reasonable to look at
the Lord Jesus Christ.

And what do we discover? We discover that there was
one occasion they came to Him and commended Him for
the fact that He did not show any favouritism. And in the
book of Leviticus, His father had given some very strict
instructions to the Levites: 'Do not pervert justice, do not
show partiality to the poor or favouritism to the great, but
judge your neighbour fairly' (Lev. 19:15).

Peter, you remember, learnt this lesson the hard way –
on the roof-top of Simon the Tanner. He fell asleep, as
many people do during their quiet times! During this
sleepy quiet time he had a vision telling him that he should
not call unclean what God had called clean, which by

interpretation meant he as a Jew was not to show favouritism. And so when he arrived at the home of Cornelius, it was very obvious what was in his mind; he said, 'I see that God does not play favourites.'

And so when we think of this powerful exhortation from James, we relate it to Jesus Christ, our standard, whose Father did not show favouritism. The very title 'Lord Jesus Christ' which James the half-brother of Jesus uses strikingly on two occasions (when beginning the epistle, and here) reminds us that He is 'Lord Jesus Christ' – Lord of all, not just some. He is Jesus the Saviour, who died for all – not just some. He is Christ the Anointed One, the Sent One, who came for all – not just some. And in fact the apostle Paul reminds us that the grace of our Lord Jesus Christ is manifested in this way, that 'though he was rich . . . he became poor so that [we] through his poverty might become rich' (2 Cor. 8:9). And so the glory of our Lord Jesus insists that we model ourselves upon Him, and do not show favouritism. That's the powerful exhortation with which James starts here.

A pointed example

James doesn't just give his exhortation at a theoretical level. He now gives a very pointed example (verses 2–4) of what he's talking about.

It probably isn't hypothetical, either. We know that the church in Jerusalem, where James was well-known and a pillar of the church, was very poor. Remember that the apostle Paul spent a considerable amount of his time raising money to go to the aid of this Jerusalem church. So if that very poor church was suddenly visited by a very ostentatiously wealthy man, what a temptation it would be to really put on a show for him!

This man (verse 2) will be wearing fine clothes, and wearing a gold ring. Some of the wealthy people in those days were so anxious to show how wealthy they were that they not only wore a ring on every finger except one, but they wore multiple rings on every finger, and even rented them for special occasions. Well, this man didn't go quite that far; he's wearing one gold ring.

The temptation of course is for the poor people sitting in this improverished church to look at this fine man coming in, and to evaluate him on purely external criteria: 'This man is wearing very fine clothes and a gold ring; he is a man of substance' – and, because he is a man of substance, deserving of special treatment.

But at the same time a shabby little fellow comes in: he's filthy dirty. And everybody says, 'He hasn't been close to a bathtub or a shower for a week! He's a mess! Where on earth can we park him?' Well, the decision is, 'Well, you go and stand over there in the corner', or, 'Well look; there's a seat here at my footstool.' If there's one thing that insulted a Jew more than anything else, it was to tell him to sit down at somebody's feet. It was like saying, 'Lick my boots!'

Now you see the prejudice that's going on here. James's point is that these Christians evaluate people by externals. They are very quick to act in prejudice. And they are opportunistic; doubtless they can see advantages in befriending a wealthy newcomer. 'Now,' says James, as he looks at this very pointed example, 'This is what you're doing: you are discriminating among yourselves. You are coming to judgemental positions about people.' And he characterises this in no uncertain terms. He says, 'This is evil thinking!'

You say, 'This doesn't seem particularly relevant to us in our churches today.' Let me just ask you a question: have you ever been tempted to think about some politician, a person in show-business, an athlete perhaps – 'Wouldn't he make a wonderful Christian?'? The chances are, in all probability, no he wouldn't! But why do we think he would make a wonderful Christian? Because it would be wonderful for us if he was a Christian! It would help our finances and our status, and we would have some ready-made credibility. That's showing favouritism, and it is discriminatory, and it can be evil.

A practical explanation

James has given us a powerful exhortation and a pointed example. Now (verses 5–7) he gives us a practical explanation. He makes three points. The first is that refusing to engage in favouritism and partiality which is evil *reminds us how God operates*.

How does God operate? Well, first of all, he tells us in verse 5 that God chooses poor people to be rich in faith. He chooses these poor people to inherit the kingdom and be rich in faith, and he reminds us that these people love Him.

If we look at people on the basis purely and simply of their external appearance, it's just possible that we might miss somebody who under the shabby clothing on the poor exterior, is actually rich in faith. A wonderful believer, a member of the kingdom; somebody who really loves the Lord.

That's the mistake that we can make; that we can miss out on the wonderful way that God chooses and enriches and uses the most unlikely people. He has a delightful way of doing things in exactly the opposite way to the way we would do them. And so James explains that you've got to be very careful how you evaluate people, for the simple reason that God sometimes chooses poor people. He calls them to the kingdom and He makes them rich in faith, and they love Him dearly and serve Him well.

This is a very appropriate word for us today. World Vision in a recent survey identified the fact that of the approximately five billion people on the face of God's earth, 2.2 billion live in destitution and dreadful poverty. Almost half the world's population are living in the lowest grades of poverty, according to our standards. And in the same survey they identified the fact that fifty per cent of the world's population is redundant. By that they mean that fifty per cent of the world's population makes no contribution to the well-being of society as a whole. They are dependant, they are needy, they are poverty-stricken. If that's the case, we'd better wake up to the fact that half the world's population, by our standards, by our external criteria, wouldn't even rate, and yet those are the ones among whom we are to work.

The second thing that he gives us here by way of explanation is that he tells us *how discriminators operate*. He says some very interesting things about what those who are discriminating against the poor are actually doing.

Verse 6: 'You are insulting the poor by discriminating against them.' We who discriminate against them insult those whom God honours. That's the first thing that he wants us to understand. The second thing that he says is this: 'Is it not the rich whom you are buttering up, who are actually exploiting poor people? You are now finding yourselves on the side of the exploiters.' And, thirdly, he says, 'Isn't it the rich people who are dragging you people into court?'

James is probably thinking about his half-brother. It wasn't the common people who dragged Him into court, who had Him done away with; it was people from the top echelons of society. Maybe James has that in mind, but he certainly is bearing in mind something that we all know is true; that in many regions of the world those who have the power are those who are persecuting the poor. And if we side with them – against the poor – then we may find ourselves siding with the persecutors.

Those people who are exploiting the poor are those who (verse 7) are also very often slandering the noble name of Him to whom you belong. So be careful that you see the poor people the way God does, and be careful that you look at the discriminators the way God does. Be careful whose side you're on.

But then the third thing that he teaches us is that we have to be aware of *where believers stand* in this whole matter. As he's already pointed out, believers are members of the kingdom of God, not of the kingdoms of this world. They march to a different drummer, they breath different air; they're different people. They love Jesus.

And notice what he talks about, here in verse 7: 'The noble name, the honourable name, of Christ'. The Christian takes upon himself or herself the name of Christ. Now, if we are members of the kingdom, if we love Jesus, if we dare to take upon ourselves the name of Christ, and in addition to that we belong to Him – then all these things are true of the believer who is poor, too, and we should look at him or her in that perspective.

The royal law

And not only that; the believer is somebody who, according to verse 8, is under the royal law.

Presumably the adjective 'royal' is related to the idea of being a member of the kingdom. What does the royal law tell us? It tells us that we are to love our neighbour as ourselves. 'But who is our neighbour?' said the man who heard Jesus say that – and he got a shock, because he heard the parable of the good Samaritan.

And so we look at this royal law, this principle of operation for those who are members of the kingdom, and we see how imperative it is that we should be operating on the basis of caring for those who are under-privileged. Notice that he adds, concerning this law, that it condemns those who break it but liberates those who keep it.

Now, just take this picture of the poor person, the person in need, the person you're tempted to think is a nuisance and isn't going to help you any at all. When you obey the law to love that person as yourself, it's remarkably liberating. It liberates you from many of your fears, it liberates you from your prejudices, it liberates you from your selfishness, and you begin to find yourself free to love and free to care.

But if you don't, you find yourself bottled up by your own selfishness, bottled up by your own greed, bottled up by your own supercilious attitude, and condemned.

And so James goes on to remind us that we are not free to be selective concerning this royal law. We are to apply it right across the board. Then he comes out with this wonderful statement at the end: 'Mercy triumphs over judgement.' I've underlined that heavily in my Bible.

Having been trained as a bank manager, I find it the easiest thing in the world to evaluate people quickly, to be critical of others and to dismiss people with alacrity. And that's why I have discovered the power of this simple message: that if I am to be a member of the kingdom and to see people as God sees them and to evaluate them as God evaluates them, and to operate under the royal law of the King which requires me to love my neighbour as myself – that to the extent that I will stop being critical and analytical and judgemental of them, but begin to be merciful and kind and generous towards them, the remarkable thing is that I find myself wonderfully liberated. And every time I refuse, I find myself in a strait-jacket of my own prejudice.

Let me ask you a couple of questions about this. It may be that we don't have a problem here in the specific area that James is talking about, but there is discrimination in the church. What about racism? And what about sexism? And what about reverse discrimination? Now, I'm simply raising those questions for you.

Faith

Now we come to the second thing here: faith. Let's look at verses 14–17.

This is the passage that gave Martin Luther a headache, because he felt that James was contradicting Paul; that James was teaching justification by works in direct contradiction of Paul's doctrine that justification is by grace through faith. Well, let's look at this.

Some assumptions
First of all, notice the assumptions that James makes here.

1. *People can be saved*. That's the first assumption.

2. *People are saved by faith*. It's very important that we underline this, because many have maligned James at this point and suggested that he doesn't believe that. He is assuming in this rhetorical question: 'Can such faith save him?', first of all, that people can be saved and, secondly, that faith is the means of salvation.

(Incidentally, the Greek word *pistis* – 'faith' – is found no less than fourteen times in these first two chapters, and fifteen times in all in the whole of James.)

3. *Faith can be phoney*. James goes further. He is assuming people can be saved, he is assuming that they are saved by faith, but he is also assuming that faith can be phoney and that, therefore, it needs to be carefully evaluated.

We are, of course, well aware of the fact that *what* we believe is of tremendous significance, but James wants to underline that *how* we believe is desperately important too. The object of our faith determines the validity of our faith; you can put minimal faith in thick ice and be safe. Conversely, you can have very big faith in very thin ice. And you will drown by faith.

What you put your faith in is of vital importance; we know that. But James is adamant that the calibre and quality of our faith is desperately important. Those are the assumptions that he makes here in the question, 'Can such faith save him?'

Some assertions
Now we look at some assertions that he makes here.

1. *Faith is dead if devoid of compassion.* That is a very powerful statement. We sing the chorus 'Trust and Obey'; we recognise that faith and obedience are the two legs on which the Christian life is lived; we are reminded of the expression in Romans, 'the obedience of faith'.

Faith is demonstrated in reality in obedience to the one in whom we have exercised faith. If we exercise faith in a Lord, the reality of our faith in a Lord is our response to His lordship in obedience. This Lord in His lordship has required us to follow His example and has required us to adhere to the royal law. Therefore, if the royal law says that I should love my neighbour, and I say, 'I have faith in the Lord of that law,' then the reality of my faith will be demonstrated in the compassion that I demonstrate in obedience to that command.

2. *Faith is dead if it is only a credal confession.* Verses 18–19 probably relate to the great statement in Deuteronomy 4:6, the beginning of the *Shema*, where the orthodox Jew, every single day, would recite these words: 'The Lord our God is one God.' James says, it is perfectly possible to say that credal confession every single morning of your life. However, if it is not born of an obedience of faith in that Lord our God who is one, it is invalid.

What a powerful word that is! But frequently we will train people to recite a creed which, of itself, is a wonderful tool for learning and a wonderful base for discovering the faith; but we also know that it is possible for us to recite it totally devoid of content. And James gives us a very striking debunking of the idea that, provided you recite a creed, you're all right. He says in effect, 'The demons can say that – the demons believe that!'

Notice the lovely expression 'the demons believe and shudder'. The word means literally 'bristle'. The demons believe so thoroughly, and are so shaken by what they believe, that it makes their hair stand on end, but who's going to say the demons are redeemed?

So James is making some very powerful assertions now.

3. *Faith and deeds are not optional*. Some people will say, 'Well, I go in for faith, and you go in for works. I'm sort of one of these passive, contemplative people, and you are a hyper-active person.' James says, 'We don't have that option; it's not either-or, it is both-and.'

Now this is very important so far as the Church's mission is concerned. Spurgeon said, 'If you want to give a hungry man a tract, wrap it in a sandwich.' Alec Motyer, in his excellent commentary on James, prefers – 'If you want to give a hungry man a sandwich, wrap it in a tract.' Well, I suppose that illustrates the different balance of these two things, but clearly there's balance there – sandwich and tract.

The mission of the Church is intended to be a ministry to the whole man. And so it isn't a case of simply saying, 'Well, there are the doers *there* and there are the passive people there.' It is a case of recognising the simple fact that when we are people of faith we will be people of action, and there will be a way of showing our faith. 'Show me your faith,' says James.

4. *Faith and actions go together*. 'You foolish man!' Now, I think either we have an actual person interrupting James while he's giving a sermon, and this is the notes from it; or he is engaging in the old Jewish way of communicating called 'diatribe'. Either way, you have an argument with somebody here.

James says, 'Do you want evidence that faith without
deeds is useless?' And he gives an example, and the example he gives is Abraham. The critical verse, as far as
Abraham is concerned, is Genesis 15:6, quoted here and
quoted by Paul: 'Abraham believed God, and it was credited to him for righteousness.'

Abraham's faith was the basis upon which righteousness
was reckoned to him. It says so in Genesis. Paul picks it up
as he insists that man is 'justified not by the works of the
law but by grace through faith'. Funnily enough, James
uses the identical expression to prove that faith and works
go together. Now, how does he do that? Well, his point is
very simple. He says, 'Abraham believed God and it was
credited to him for righteousness.' The question is, how   *
do we know he believed? And the answer is, by what he
did.

The history of Abraham is very straightforward. In
Genesis 12 we're told that God called him to go to a place,
and didn't tell him where it was, and he went. In Genesis
15 we're told that God covenanted with him, and he
believed. In Genesis 22 we're told – and this is what James
zeros in on particularly – that God commanded that he
sacrifice his son Isaac in whom all the covenant blessings
were locked up, and Abraham showed that he was ready
to obey. And when God reached out and wanted to be a
companion to Abraham, Abraham responded.

So James's conclusion is very simple and very straightforward. He says, 'If you want evidence that Abraham
was justified by faith, and you want to know that the faith
was there, the evidence was this: when he was called he
obeyed, when there was offer of a covenant he believed,
when he was commanded he did what he was told, and
when God reached out to him in companionship he
responded, and all these are evidences of his faith.'

Abraham gives us ample evidence that faith without
deeds is useless. James also tells us that Abraham's faith

was – notice the word – *completed* by what he did (in verse 22). Does that word 'completed' ring a bell? It should – a very faint one, from as far back as yesterday! Check in chapter one, and you'll see that it is there.

James's other conclusion is that faith and works work together. Interesting word here – we're familiar with the expression 'we are workers together with God'; well, this is the verb that relates to the noun: faith and works working together. There's one other example he gives – the example of Rahab the prostitute.

Notice that, characteristically, he's using extremes here. He has just referred to a reputable man. Now, he not only refers to a woman, which was unusual in those days, but to a disreputable woman.

This particular lady, Rahab, had the oldest profession in the world, as they say. When the children of Israel came and spied out Jericho, you remember that she had a word with the spies, who identified themselves to her. She said, 'Listen, I don't have any doubts – the Lord your God is God in heaven above and in earth below.' She believed! How do we know that she believed? She stuck her neck out! And she rescued those men from certain death.

And so James comes up with two very simple illustrations of the fact that faith and actions go together. Abraham, the reputable man; Rahab, the disreputable woman. And he says that as the body without the Spirit is dead, so faith that doesn't demonstrate itself in compassion and concern and companionship and courage, is not real faith at all. He's not saying we are justified by these things – we are justified by grace through faith – but the evidence that our faith is saving faith is that it works. And in the same way, he says that a body without the Spirit is a corpse, so a faith that doesn't show itself in lively activities of faith is dead.

3. Tongues of Fire, and Heavenly Wisdom
(James 3:1–17)

Tongues of fire

I have to start with an apology. In our last Bible study, I left you with your tongues hanging out! For we came to James 3:1–12, and introduced the topic of the tongue but didn't have time to get into it.

So let me lead you through these first twelve verses of chapter 3, before we move on to today's study.

As you read 3:1 you will recall that James has already introduced the topic of the tongue in 1:26: 'If anyone . . . does not keep a tight rein on his tongue . . .' He is at great pains to remind us that true faith demonstrates itself in behaviour. He points out strongly that our behaviour is often demonstrated in how we use our tongues. So this is a very challenging passage of Scripture indeed.

The tongue is the tool of the teacher
First of all (verse 1) James reminds us that the tongue is the tool of the teacher.

In his day, a teacher was called 'Rabbi', and the word 'Rabbi' meant literally 'My Great One'. So to be a teacher was to be a person who held a prestigious position. Understandably, it was an often sought-after position. In our day too, of course, we know that the person with the gift of teaching is a highly privileged person.

The apostle Paul talks about being a steward of the mysteries of God. By that, he means that things have been revealed to him that people uninitiated in Christ are not aware of at all. But he recognises that this is not so that he might simply use them for his own benefit, but that as a steward he might use them for the benefit of others.

One of the great challenges that I live with constantly is that, in my calling as a preacher and a teacher, God, for reasons known only to Himself, has opened my eyes to truth; that He has done so not in order that I might simply live in the good of it but in order that I might make it available to other people. And I often reflect that living in today's world I'm surrounded by people who live in darkness. The god of this world has blinded their minds, and for reasons known only to Himself, God has placed me in their midst. And I'm a steward of the mysteries. To be a teacher is prestigious, to be a teacher is to be privileged; to be a teacher means that you live in a very precarious position indeed.

Consequently those who would presume to be teachers should be very, very careful indeed, because their tool is their tongue. And the tongue is a very slippery customer indeed.

I think we should take this very much to heart, because in the Church of Jesus Christ today, as in all ages, we sometimes tend to put people in positions of teaching responsibility who perhaps ought not to be there. And sometimes, perhaps, for motives that are less than honourable, we want to be teaching when we may not be guarding ourselves as we ought. Remember that 'those to whom much is given will have much required of them'. The teacher has received much in terms of privilege, in terms of prestige, in terms of truth revealed, in terms of immense responsibility – but let's be very careful how we handle this whole business.

You see, the problem is that the tongue is a tool that can be used to inform and inspire, but also to inflame and insult. And therein lies our problem.

The tongue is the measure of the mature

In verse 2, James, with characteristic skill, makes use of prolific illustrations. He thinks of the horse with a bit in its mouth, of the great ship out at sea, of a little spark setting off a great forest fire.

So, he says, this little member of our body that so often we don't regard as particularly significant, is in fact of phenomenal importance; because, unless it is controlled, it can lead to all kinds of disaster and do terrible damage. Conversely, this little member, if it is properly controlled, will lead to a control of the whole of life.

Therefore, the tongue is a measure of the mature. If you find somebody whose tongue is out of control, you have found somebody who is spiritually, emotionally, or intellectually immature. If on the other hand you have found somebody who can speak wisely, judiciously, carefully, positively and helpfully, you have found somebody who is mature.

This is what John Wesley wrote in his book *Spiritual Awakening*:

> Love constrains the believer to converse not only with a strict regard to truth but with artless sincerity and genuine simplicity, as one in whom there is no guile, and, not content with abstaining from all such expressions as are contrary to justice or truth, he endeavours to refrain from every unloving word, either to a present or absent person. In all his conversation he aims either to improve himself in knowledge, or virtue, or to make

those with whom he converses some way wiser, or better, or happier than they were before.

I think we agree that if we come across people whose tongues are used like that, we have come across a mature person.

The tongue is the weapon of the wicked
It is like a forest fire (verse 6). Notice that in his illustration of a tiny spark setting a whole forest on fire, he goes back a little and talks about the origin of the spark. Where does that spark come from?

He tells us (verse 6) that the spark is set on fire by hell. The word used is *gehenna*. Those of you who are familiar with the history of ancient Jerusalem will know that there's a deep valley on the west side of Mount Zion, and in that deep valley it was customary in ancient times for the god Moloch to be worshipped, by – among other methods – the offering of infants to him in blazing furnaces. But in later times, in the days when our Lord and James were in Jerusalem, Gehenna became the city rubbish dump. They were always burning rubbish there. It was a gloomy, smelly, horrible place.

Thus James is using most powerful language here, when he says that the spark that gets into the tongue is something that comes from this dark, horrible, hellish place. He's talking about it being devilish.

More: he says that this spark that starts in Gehenna produces 'a world of evil'. That is an interesting expression. Perhaps what he means is that all the aspects of the evil world are to be found in the tongue – all that is vile, all that is reprehensible, all that is unacceptable about a world system that is antithetical to God, can be found in it. Set on fire in Gehenna, that spark of godlessness, that spark of rebellion, that spark of obscenity, is to be found there. And he goes on in verse 6 (rather mixing his metaphors!) to show that this spark can stain the whole body.

So when we think in terms of what the tongue is capable of, we recognise that it can become a weapon of wickedness. We're very good at making excuses for our words, aren't we? We're very good at pardoning the things that we say and the way that we say them. And perhaps what we need to remember is what James says here about it being like a forest fire. Have you ever said something, or had something said of you, that was later discovered to be untrue? The damage can't be undone. Often relationships are spoiled by it. I think we tend to minimise the wickedness of this weapon called the tongue when it is used improperly.

It is like a half-tamed wild animal (verses 7 and 8). Now the picture changes from a forest fire to a zoo, full of half-tamed wild animals. Isn't it interesting that 'man' – that is, male and female – was given in Genesis 1 the commission to rule and reign over God's creation? One of the things that we're required to do now, because it is a fallen creation, is to tame – to train – the animal kingdom.

Man has had considerable success in taming and training all sorts of creatures. And when you think of the tremendous ability that man has to take the animals and to train them and direct them and tame them, it's a strange irony that man with this remarkable God-given capability can't tame his tongue. He can't bring it under control.

Consequently it becomes a 'restless evil'. 'Restless' is one of James's favourite words. He's talked about there being instability and disorder. We'll see that in 3:16, and remember that right at the very beginning he talked about the double-minded man being unstable. James has a sense of disorderliness appearing everywhere. And he sees this disorderliness in the tongue.

So it's a very gloomy picture that James is painting for us here.

It is like a polluted well (verses 9–12). Nobody could ever accuse James of being a dull speaker! If it's illustrations you want, he even illustrates his illustrations! They come tumbling out on top of each other here.

He talks about the tongue as being like a polluted well; how incongruous it would be, if we went to a well that sometimes gave us a bucket of fresh water and sometimes a bucket of salt water. That would be most inconsistent behaviour for a well. And it's inconsistent behaviour for a tongue to be eulogising God the Father and then to turn round and distress that which is made in the very image of God the Father.

I think one of the most important things for us all to remember is one of the cardinal doctrines of the Christian faith: that man is made in the image of God, and that the way that we treat man is very often a marked reflection of our attitude towards God.

James goes on to remind us that the fruit of a tree demonstrates its root.

This is one of the oldest principles imaginable. You can tie all kinds of things to a fruit tree but it won't make any difference to what the tree is. What the tree is will manifest itself in fruit, and all kinds of external accretions will make no difference whatsoever – tying apples on a pear tree does not make a pear tree an apple tree. And coming up with elaborate phraseology and using all kinds of sophisticated theological jargon will not alter the fact that if my tongue is not in tune with my Creator, there's still wickedness there.

Now, having painted this terrible picture of the tongue (and remember James's point: that if we are truly of the faith, our faith will be demonstrated in activity, and one of our major activities is the activity of the tongue) we are now left with this overwhelming problem: how on earth are we going to cope with this wretched little member?

Will Rogers, that wonderful, earthy, philosopher-comedian in the United States of America said, 'We should so live that we won't be ashamed to sell the family parrot to the town gossip.' Well, that's a great rule of thumb. The problem is, we need help from James to find out how to do it!

Which brings us to the third section of our study of James.

Wisdom (3:13–17)

Now we turn to chapter 3:13, where James immediately asks another pointed, abrupt question: 'Who is wise and understanding among you? Let him show it.' It is a characteristic expression of James. In 2:18 he says: If you talk about faith, show it to me in your deeds! Here he says: You say you have wisdom; all right, show me!

The ever-practical, ever-down-to-earth James won't let us away with cliches. He won't let us away with noble expression. He says (verses 13–18 – note, in passing, the recurrence of 'disorder' in verse 16) that if there is wisdom, true wisdom, it is going to be visible and it is going to be tangible.

A problem of the heart

James has pointed out to us that bad behaviour of the tongue will be indicative of immaturity and inconsistency in our Christian profession and performance. He has not yet dealt with the question of how we cope with this wretched member, but he is now going to show us that the problem with the tongue is basically a problem of the heart, and that if the heart is put right the tongue will begin to behave differently.

We have a wonderful rule of thumb from the Scriptures in Luke: it is out 'of the abundance of the heart' that the mouth speaks (Luke 6:45, AV). When we talk about the heart, we're not just talking about a blood-pump. We're talking about the inner resources of our being, from which spring the motives and the desires that will put our members into operation.

James is going to tell us that unless the heart is controlled by wisdom, the tongue will be hopelessly out of control: that is his line of reasoning.

The good life

Notice that he talks about 'wisdom and understanding'. Then he points out to us that this wisdom and understanding will be demonstrated by our living a good life (verse 13).

Let me first of all define 'the good life'.

There's a television programme in the United States called 'Life-styles of the Rich and Famous'.[1] It's about people who are extremely wealthy and basically have no idea what to do with their wealth. They simply dissipate it on all kinds of extravagant, insignificant things. I must admit that I have never managed to sit through a whole programme.

There's a lot of confusion about what 'the good life' is. Have you noticed how the politicians are always talking about the quality of life?

Our ethicists now talk about 'the quality of life' where we used to talk about 'the sanctity of life' (incidentally, take care: as soon as you agree to the switch from sanctity of life to quality of life, you've opened the door for all kinds of problems such as abortion and euthanasia).

Whenever we talk about 'the quality of life' or 'the good life' in purely secular terms, we may be heading for deep trouble. And what James calls 'the good life' is far removed from what passes, in secular human terms, for the good life today.

The word 'good' used here is *kalēs*, and it means 'good'
in the sense of 'lovely'. So if we're going to make a
contrast between this good life, and what passes for the
good life, let me suggest to you that it is the difference
between something that is intrinsically beautiful, and
something that is simply superficially glamorous. Now
there's a difference! The good life that many people are
looking for falls into the category of superficially glamorous. But the good life that is the result of wisdom that is
deeply embedded in the heart and demonstrates itself in
behaviour, is not glamorous, it's beautiful.

The good life that people talk about in secular, human
terms usually relates to *possessions*. Have you noticed
how the words 'good' and 'goods' are related, and that
very often people think that 'goods' equals 'the good life'?
And that if you have such a *good* life that you not only
have *goods*, but then you can become really extravagant
and spend your time on goodies then you've got the good
life? That's the secular thinking.

I'm very happy to have goods, and I am not adverse to
goodies; but I do worry about the idea that our good life is
determined by these possessions. And what James is telling us is this: it's not so much possessions as expressions of
deep-rooted wisdom that produce the good life, that will
help among other things to control the tongue, which
among other things will produce Christian maturity.

When he speaks of 'the good life', James is not interested in the extravagant, he is interested in the significant.
And therein lies the problem – just getting people to think
of what is significant. It's easy to persuade people to think
of what is extravagant and glamorous; but getting them to
think in terms of what is intrinsically beautiful, that's
hard.

James makes a marked distinction between the two.
He's talking about the *kalēs* life – the good, lovely, fine,
intrinsically valuable life.

The beginning of wisdom

Now, how do we develop this good life? As we've already seen, the answer is through the acquisition of wisdom.

James differentiates between two different kinds of wisdom. He talks about 'the wisdom that comes from heaven' (verse 17) and explains it; but in marked contrast in verse 15 he talks about 'the "wisdom" that does not come down from heaven'.

What do we mean by the wisdom that comes down from heaven? Well, Scripture tells us in Proverbs 2:1 – that 'the fear of the Lord is the beginning of wisdom'. In other words, it is only when we begin to understand who the Lord is, and what role He plays in our lives, that we're even close to the beginning of wisdom.

Let's be careful at this point. There are many highly educated people who have little or no perception of the Lord. We should not therefore confuse high education with spiritual wisdom that is going to touch a person's heart and produce in them the life of beauty and quality and significance, and the attitudes that accompany it, so that – among other things – their tongues will be controlled.

Human wisdom sometimes lets us down. In 1958 the Chairman of IBM said: 'The world can use about five computers.' In 1899, Charles Duewel, the director of the USA Patent Office said: 'Everything that can be invented has been invented.' In 1927, Harry Warner, of Hollywood's Warner Brothers, said: 'Who wants to hear actors talk anyway?' And President Grover Cleveland of the USA said, in the early twentieth century, 'Sensible and responsible women don't want to vote.'

Well – it's very nice to have these educated, helpful people around! But, while we do not fall into the trap of the old Fundamentalists, who were anti-intellectual, we also recognise there's all the difference in the world between the wisdom that comes from heaven and even the best of human education. The two need not necessarily be confused.

Well now, what about this beginning of wisdom? What about this wisdom that begins with acknowledging who the Lord is? It blossoms into 'understanding' (verse 13). The word 'understanding' means 'well-informed'. So, in other words, he's saying that the wisdom that comes from the fear of the Lord begins to inform a person about all aspects of life. The Lord is integrated into all dimensions of his or her being.

Sometimes we have a problem here, because we keep the Lord and spiritual things in a watertight compartment and keep everything else separate and distinct. But James is insisting that this wisdom that begins with the fear of the Lord permeates every dimension of our being.

I remember talking to a friend of mine who was going to South Africa and, as I had spent some time in South Africa, he asked me if I would brief him on my understanding of that wonderful country and the terrible problems that it's going through. When he came back, he told me, 'I can't believe how wrong you are about South Africa. You have got it all wrong.' And he outlined his understanding of it to me.

I listened very carefully to what he had to say, and then I said to him, 'You've talked about politics, and you've talked about race, and you've talked about economics, and you've talked about sociology, and it seems to me that from all these vantage points probably you can make a good case on what you're saying. But I have one question. Where does your theology fit into all this?' And he said, 'Oh, I haven't got around to that yet.'

I said to him, 'You don't "get around" to that: you *start* there. You start with your theology – your heavenly wisdom – and you begin to integrate that into your anthropology, and your psychology – you begin to integrate that into all dimensions of your life, even your politics.'

One of the great needs is for men and women to begin to derive their wisdom from above and then become well-informed, so that it begins to permeate every aspect of their lives.

Seven virtues of wisdom
When it does, it will bloom in seven virtues. Now, notice exactly what these virtues are (verse 17).

1. The word *pure* is related to the word for 'holiness'; it means 'free from blemish'.

2. The word *peaceable* means 'peace-loving', and 'peace-making'. If you want to see that James wasn't just theorising in this regard, look up two passages in Acts – chapter 15 where he presided over the council of Jerusalem and had a great peace-making role there, and chapter 21 where he was functioning in a similar capacity.

So you can tell the people who are deriving wisdom from above, who are integrating it into their lives, so that it is becoming a dominating factor in their thinking about life; because their life begins to be increasingly holy, they become increasingly peace-loving and committed to peace-making.

3. They become *considerate*. The word here is 'accepting, flexible, willing to yield gently, amenable' – not the kind of people who will say, 'My mind is made up, don't confuse me with facts.' That is always a problem in our churches.

4. The fourth characteristic is *submissive*. That means, persuasive in communication, but also capable of being persuaded.

5. *Merciful*. That means, having a concern and a sensitivity to those who are hurting. Heavenly wisdom

understands people's needs, it checks on helplessness and begins to reach out fruitfully towards these people.

6. *Impartial*. Here again is one of James's favourite themes: 'not in two minds'.

7. And lastly, *sincere*. The word literally means, 'not hypocritical'. You will know that the Greek word for 'hypocrite' means, literally, a play-actor. The actors in those days would hide behind a mask, and their own feelings were irrelevant because the mask would convey the role they were playing. The hypocrite is the person who lives behind the mask.

Now, just look at those qualities, and ask yourself a question – what would happen in our own church, if instead of our tongues wagging the way they do, our hearts were touched with wisdom from above in such a way that it was integrated in all aspects of our lives? So that it began to bloom in purity, in peace-loving, peace-making attitudes, in accepting, amenable, flexible, yielding, persuadable, persuasive, sensitive, committed, sincere, open, honest living? Do you think it would make any difference? I suspect it would!

Wisdom produces meekness
Look now, back in verse 13, at the attitude that wisdom produces. We're actually working backwards. We started with the good life that comes from wisdom. But the wisdom produces the humility, and the humility produced the deeds, and the deeds produce the good life.

What is this 'humility that comes from wisdom?' The word is 'meekness'. That's a word that we don't like very much. Have you noticed that? The reason we don't like meekness very much, is it rhymes with weakness. But it is not the same as weakness. It is strength that chooses not to exert itself. Humility is not the kind of humility that pretends to be terribly submissive, and terribly persuaded, but really isn't; it is a genuine, realistic evaluation of the self, and is prepared to respond and to yield to what is going on.

In 1:21, James uses the word 'meekness' again, concerning our attitude to the Word of God. Calvin says that that means we have 'a mind disposed to learn' from the Scriptures – but a meekness towards God as well, a humble attitude towards God.

I always feel that when it comes to our relationship with God, we've an awful lot to be humble about. Therefore humility and meekness would seem to be very appropriate indeed. They are the result, of course, of heavenly wisdom. Weakness, meekness towards the Word, meekness towards God and meekness towards people. The person who suggests they have 'arrived' is a stranger to meekness, and the person who suggests they know it all doesn't know an awful lot about the wisdom that comes from above.

Wisdom leads to acts of righteousness
Now we put all this together. This wisdom that comes from above, that starts with the fear of the Lord, is integrated in all areas of life, produces these virtues, and all of these virtues develop an attitude within us of meekness towards God and towards His Word and towards people, a genuine humility, and then moves into action (verse 18).

So what kind of humble activities are going to be seen, instead of the kind of activities of the tongue that rip and ruin?

There is going to be 'sowing in peace', and a great deal of order in life, because peace means (in Augustine's definition) 'the tranquillity of order'. There's going to be a great concern for putting things right. And the result of that is 'a harvest of righteousness', which means right living, right behaviour, treating people, and living rightly before God. What a crop! What a harvest!

Guarding against earthly wisdom. However, we have
had the development of the good life described, but this
good life has to be defended. While there is wisdom from
heaven above, there is also another kind of wisdom. And
this other kind of wisdom – 'earthly, unspiritual, of the
devil' (verse 15) – has to be guarded against.

The problem with much earthly wisdom is that it often
has a lot to commend it. It is often good, sound common
sense. But the trouble with a lot of good, sound common
sense is that it makes an awful lot of sense, but is totally
devoid of any spiritual understanding.

Let me give you an example:

We know perfectly well that the Spirit of God sometimes calls people to go and do things, but the unbelieving
family, using very sound common sense, being highly
practical and very realistic, say, 'That is a dumb, stupid,
crazy thing to do.' It's unearthly and it's unspiritual – it
has nothing to do with the Spirit of God. And the tragedy
of it is that if he's not careful it can be devilish. Yes – even
good, loving family people can be responsible for wisdom
being pumped into us that is purely secular, that has
nothing to do with the Spirit, and manages to achieve the
devil's end.

Remember what happened to Peter. Peter was emi-
nently sensible when he said, 'Lord, if it's going to be
dangerous for You to go to Jerusalem – and we love You,
we don't want You in danger – the obvious thing is, don't
go to Jerusalem.' But Jesus turned on him and said –
what? 'Well, thank you very much for that very sensible,
good solid advice'? No, He didn't; He said, 'Get behind
me, Satan.' Because sometimes, totally common-sense
arguments from well-meaning people will achieve purely
secular, humanistic, devilish ends. That is why it is so
utterly imperative that we keep in step with the Spirit:
wisdom from above.

So we guard ourselves against wrong information, by testing it by the Scriptures. But not only that.

Guarding against wrong attitudes. In verse 16 James points out that the wrong advice, being estranged from heavenly wisdom and out of touch with the Word of God, being out of touch with the Spirit of God, being out of step with the divine purposes, can mean that you finish up being inordinately concerned about yourself (that's what 'envy' means there) and totally committed to looking out for Number One.

A man in America called Ronald Ringer stayed in the best-seller lists for a long time with three books. They were called *Looking Out for Number One*, *Winning Through Intimidation*, and *Restoring the American Dream*. The equivalents would be bestsellers in Britain too, because in our own sinful hearts, that's basically what we're all interested in. Looking out for Number One, winning by any means, and restoring our own dream of the good life.

But we have to remember that there is another wisdom that militates against these things. There is an alternative; to commit ourselves completely to heavenly wisdom, letting it permeate every area of our lives, seeing it produce its virtues, developing a humble life-style, and working humbly in the will of God. And the sheer power of this, among other things, is going to help us control our tongue, which is one of our biggest problems.

1. Insomniac readers wishing to investigate this programme will find that several ITV companies transmit it as part of all-night programme schedules.

4. Warfare, and the Will of God: Promise, Prayer and Problem People (James 4:1–5:20)

As this is the concluding study, and the last time that I will speak to you here during this Convention, I think it will be appropriate for me to express my deep appreciation to you for the invitation to be here, for the patience with which you have responded to all the vicissitudes of the elements this week, and for the very warm response that you have given to Jill and me while we've been here.

We come now to chapter 4. You'll remember of course that James is particularly concerned that our faith should be visible as well as viable, that it should be tangible, that there should be evidence. What he's saying over and over again is, 'Show me! Don't just say, don't just profess – perform!'

He's been dealing with various ways in which we show our faith. He's given us a very helpful insight into the secret of living a faith that works, and showed us that all the time we need to be determining which wisdom we will listen to, and what will be the operative dynamic in our lives. He's showed us that, among many other things, when we begin to operate on the basis of the heavenly wisdom, there will be a real sense of peace in our lives.

Remember, the root meaning of the word 'peace' in the Old and the New Testament is 'a sense of order'. Over and over again, James has been talking about disorderliness, instability, chaos; and in an unstable, chaotic world, what a delightful thing it is to find people of peace, whose lives are in order but who also are concerned about bringing order. They are peace-loving, peaceable and they are peace-makers.

Warfare (4:1–12)

With all that in mind, he now asks a typical James question: 'What causes fights and quarrels among you?' (verse 1).

That's a good question! It's one thing to talk about operating on the wisdom from above, and producing a peaceable life and a harvest of righteousness. But the simple fact of the matter as far as this very practical man is concerned is this: we can talk about peace until we're blue in the face, but we have to face up to the fact that war and strife and tension and violence and disintegration and disorderliness are on every hand. We can ignore it if we want to, but we do so at our peril.

Did you know that at this very moment there are twenty-five wars in progress? And did you know that these twenty-five wars have so far claimed in excess of three million lives, and that 80 per cent of those people are civilians? Did you know that the developing countries spend four times as much on arms as they do on health care, even though 20 per cent of their children die before the age of five? Are you aware of the fact that the USA and the USSR spend 1.5 billion dollars every single day on military defence? And did you know that since the end of the Second World War in 1945, seventeen million people have been killed in wars, rebellions and uprisings? That's almost half the total of all the people killed in World War Two. Are you aware of the fact that right at this moment, while we sit in this delightful secluded corner of God's earth, nuclear arsenals are being built that represent twenty-six thousand times the explosive force of all the armaments used in World War Two?

So James asks a good question, and I wonder how he would ask it if he lived today.

And what about the wars and rebellions that are taking place in families? And what about the disintegration in marriage? Perhaps the thing that he is really concerned about is, what about the squabbling and the quarrelling and the schismatic behaviour that goes on in the Church of God?

Now, it's all very well for us to talk about heavenly wisdom, it's all very well for us to talk about 'marching to the drum-beat of heaven', and how this produces a peace-loving, orderly, peace-making life-style; but the fact of the matter is, not only do we have international conflict and family breakdown and marital discord, but very often the life in our church fellowships is abysmal. And we need to recognise that this is the case.

We need to admit the problem (4:1)
I think Christians in the community of believers are expert at denying the tension is there, or hoping it will go away, rather than asking the hard question, 'What causes the fighting and the quarrelling and the squabbling and the schismatic behaviour that is all too often prevalent?'

But we need to admit that the problem exists, approach it with great care, and ask the questions that James is asking.

We need to analyse the problem (4:1–6)
Having admitted the problem, James then, with characteristic openness, begins to analyse the problem. It's a
solid principle. In all areas of life, if there's a problem,
admit it, and when you've admitted it, analyse it.

James isn't like a lot of preachers who just ask the
question and never get around to answering it! Having
asked his question, he answers it immediately: 'What
causes fights and quarrels among you? Don't they come
from your desires that battle within you?'

The pleasure principle (4:1)
We've already come across this word, 'desire'. The
Authorised Version translated it 'lusts', which is a little
unfortunate because the word used here is not necessarily
a negative one. There are perfectly legitimate desires that
God has planted in us, though James is very careful to
point out that those perfectly legitimate desires that God
has planted within us can become warped and twisted, and
can become the agents of devilish activity.

He does not only talk about desires; in verse 2 he talks
about wants, and later in verse 2, about coveting.

The word translated 'pleasure' here, or 'desire', is the
word from which we get 'hedonism' – that's a very interesting word. A well-known psychologist in America,
Daniel Yankelovich,[1] polled the population of the United
States, and found that whereas a few decades ago the
prevailing ethos of American society was a sense of duty,
the situation has now been totally reversed, often because
those who lived by a sense of duty felt themselves abused
by others. The reaction has spawned a new, dominating
ethos. In place of a sense of duty, we now have 'duty to
myself; I owe it to myself'.

Yankelovich says that the new ethos has produced rampant hedonism – the belief that one owes it to oneself to

experience everything that gives pleasure. And he goes on to say that this rampant hedonism will lead inevitably to the disintegration of the society; and he is extremely gloomy about the future.

I want to suggest to you that when a secular psychologist and pollster begins to point this out to us – that when people lose a sense of duty and put in its place a duty to themselves, it will lead to the disintegration of society – we had better listen, and listen hard. For if there's one community of people in the midst of a fracturing community that needs to be different, it is the Church of Jesus Christ.

James, addressing believers, says, 'Now, the fighting and the squabbling that goes on among you is directly attributable to the same kind of attitude.' And he goes on to develop the theme. This hedonism, or whatever term we want to use, is producing all kinds of problems; of course it is! Because if I am in a community of people and I'm only interested in myself and in nobody else, it's perfectly obvious what's going to happen: I am going to become so dominated by my utter intrinsic self-ism and selfishness that I will have no time for anybody else. And when others' self-interest collides with my self-interest, it's inevitable what's going to happen – they'll be squabbles and they'll be fights.

We see it internationally and we see it nationally; and we see it in families and we see it in marriages; and we see it in our fellowships.

James says, 'Let's analyse this problem.' At the root of it is the pleasure principle: these desires, wants, and covetousness that are evidence of utter self-centredness. Alec Motyer says, 'It is at root no more than the existence in each of us of a self-centred heart and a controlling spirit of self-interest.'

But now James goes on to point out another reason for this problem of fighting within and among believers.

The prayer problem (4:2–3)

In verse 3, we find the same word 'pleasures'. Isn't it interesting that James wrote this so long ago and yet is so up to date!

Now, what is the prayer problem here? Well, I want to suggest that there are three problems related to prayer that will engender the strife among believers.

The first problem is *prayerlessness*. 'You do not have because you do not ask.'

Quite frankly, it is fairly easy for believers to live their church life purely on the basis of self-effort, self-assertion and self-interest. And you don't need to pray to operate on any, or all, of those principles.

Think of how your church operates. Is it operating on the basis of self-effort, self-assertion and self-interest? Or is there a higher, nobler objective – to begin to discover what the will of God is, and to begin to identify with the plan of God, and to live in the power of God and produce a Church that is explicable only in terms of divine intervention in human affairs? Maybe part of the problem is prayerlessness.

The second problem is *inappropriate prayer*.

'You quarrel and fight. You do not have because you do not ask, and when you do ask you do not receive because you ask with wrong motives.'

Sometimes our prayers end with that lovely little phrase 'for Jesus' sake', but it has nothing to do with Jesus' sake; it's for our sake. And it may be that our prayers are made legitimate in our thinking because we say 'for Christ's sake', but in actual fact what we're really concerned with is not the honour of Christ, or the extension of His kingdom; we're not particularly concerned with the hallowing of His name or the doing of His will as it is in heaven; what we are really concerned about is self-interest.

If you have a church full of people, most of whom don't come to a prayer meeting, with a small minority who do come to the prayer meeting but are praying wrongly, it really is no surprise if you begin to get all kinds of tension. That's what James says.

A third problem might be what we would call *an unanswered prayer*: 'When you ask you do not receive . . .'

Why? 'Because you ask with wrong motives.'

You often hear about unanswered prayers. It seems to me that on the contrary there are three answers to prayer: 'Yes', 'No' and 'You've got to be kidding'. I'll leave that profound thought with you and move on!

We're analysing the problem of why there is so much tension, so much strife. The pleasure problem; the prayer problem; and now a third aspect of the problem.

The priority problem (4:4)

Verse 4: 'You adulterous people'. Now he's really taking the gloves off, isn't he?

The term 'adulterous' does not necessarily mean that they're engaging in sexual immorality; he's simply picking up a familiar Old Testament picture. What he's saying in effect is that God's people sometimes claim to be betrothed to Christ, but have actually gone off with other lovers. They've got their priorities wrong. Instead of it being a friendship with God, it is a friendship with the world.

We have something of a problem here, because our definitions of worldliness vary so much. What does it mean, to have friendship with the world in place of friendship with God?

I think we need to be very careful here. We do have a problem with our definitions of 'worldliness', and you will find, particularly if you travel among the church community world-wide, that some of our definitions of worldliness don't stand up in other segments of the Christian community.

The remarkable thing, however, is that the Bible is actually quite explicit on what constitutes worldliness: it is the lust of the flesh, the lust of the eyes and the pride of life. And all these things are going to pass away.

It is perfectly possible to abstain from beer all your life, and yet be riddled with the lust of the flesh, the lust of the eyes or the pride of life.

So when we think in terms of worldliness, what we've got to decide is this: is God our friend, or are our desire for position (the pride of life), and possession and passions – (the lust of the flesh and the lust of the eyes) the dominating factors? If those are my chief concerns, and if everybody in the fellowship is like that, everything will be wonderful! Until your passions and my passions collide, or your position challenges my position, or your possessions are better than my possessions. And then all kinds of tensions will result.

There has to be something grander than this, and there is. It's the love of God.

And so what is the priority?

There's an antagonism between God and the world; there's a mutually exclusive friendship and enmity. It's either-or. Either we are motivated by the Spirit, or we are motivated by intrinsic selfishness.

So these are the problems that cause the fightings and the feudings among us.[2]

The pride problem (4:6)

Verse 6: 'God opposes the proud, but gives grace to the humble.'

If I insist on exalting myself in the fellowship of believers, there are others who will accept it as their God-given responsibility to bring me down. If on the other hand I insist on humbling myself (the word is literally 'lay myself low before people': so, better, if I am honest and open and giving to them, and tell them what is really going on inside me, and be perfectly frank with them) it's very difficult for them to knock me down, because I've put myself down. And God will raise me up.

But if you get a church with a lot of proud, arrogant people who are becoming increasingly hard and embittered and committed to their own way of doing things, it's only a matter of time until you're going to have all kinds of problems.

Now, let's remind ourselves of what James is saying. He's saying, 'If you want to show me your faith, show me your works; if you want to show me your works, one of the works that we can anticipate is that you'll be a very peace-loving, peaceable, peace-making person.'

But you do this in the midst of all kinds of tension and conflict, and we need to identify these conflicts and tensions, and we need to ask ourselves a question: 'Why are they there?' Then we can look into Scripture, and we'll find out why they're there: because very often the people are committed to their own pleasures, and their own pride, and their own priorities, with all kinds of prayer problems thrown in.

We need to address the problem (4:7–10)
In these verses we encounter some of the fifty-plus commands to be found in James's 108 verses.

'Submit yourselves then to God', 'Resist the devil and he will flee from you', 'Come near to God and he will come near to you', 'Wash your hands, you sinner', 'Purify your hearts, you double-minded', 'Grieve', 'Mourn', 'Wail', 'Change your laughter to mourning', 'Change your joy to gloom', 'Humble yourselves before the Lord, and he will lift you up.'

That'll keep us going for a while!

Grace to appropriate and commands to obey

There are two things to notice here. Firstly, as we begin to address in our own hearts the problem that so often will engender strife in our marriages, families, churches or wherever it might be, we need to recognise that we have grace available to us to equip us to deal with the problem (verse 6). One thing you can count on is grace – grace to deal with all that is required of you.

But secondly, remember that the Christian life always operates on two tracks. There is the *grace* that God supplies which we appropriate, and there are the *commands* that God gives us which we obey.

Have you noticed how our temperament determines, to a very large extent, which aspect of spiritual truth we latch on to? There are some very relaxed, free-and-easy people, who are great at trusting, expecting, depending. They expect to do what God has commanded them to do.

On the one hand, there are very detailed, organised, goal-setting people, with ultimate, immediate, measurable goals. They carry slide-rules, stop-watches, computers – as they rush past you can hear them going 'tick-tick, tick-tick-tick'! Those are the kind of people who make lists of those fifty-plus commands in James. They get out their computers and stop-watches, and they say: 'I've got twenty-four hours in the day and there are fifty commands here; fifty into twenty-four – okay, where's my clipboard? Tick-tick-tick-tick.' Well, to those people let me remind you there is grace available.

And on the other hand, there are those people who know grace is available, and they haven't checked out a thing. They haven't even bothered reading the commands. They're just trusting God in His grace to do it! Well, let me remind those people that there are some commands and that the commands are to be taken seriously.

There's always a balance to be found. The old hymn puts it perfectly – 'Trust and obey'. We don't have the choice between them. Whichever comes naturally to you, ignore it, and concentrate on the other one!

I don't think we need to make any comment here about the specific commands in our passage, but I want to make just a very simple application of this. If there are problems in your family, humble yourself before God and admit it, analyse the problem before God on the basis of what this says, seek the grace of God to empower you to begin to rectify the problem, and then start meticulously being obedient. Do likewise if there's a problem in your marriage, or problems in your church. And if you do that, you begin to demonstrate the reality of your faith.

We move on.

The will of God (4:13–17)

James is now expounding his expression 'humble yourselves'. The problem is that sometimes we don't humble ourselves very much because we are rather arrogant and self-sufficient; and we make our plans (verse 13).

It's an attitude that says, in effect, 'I've all the time in the world! I can go anywhere I wish. I can do my own thing. I will carry on business, and I'll make money.' And it's an attitude that is prevalent in our society.

But is the same attitude infiltrating the Church? The answer has to be 'Yes.' And it is not the attitude of humility.

What's wrong with this attitude? It overlooks some very simple facts. We don't even know what will happen tomorrow. The person who casually and arrogantly goes around saying, 'I've all the time in the world; I'll go anywhere I wish, I'll do my own thing and I'll make a bundle,' is overlooking something. He or she doesn't realise that they are 'like the mist that appears for a little while and then vanishes'.

It's hard to see how anybody could ever be dominated by self-interest and self-assertion, when the Scriptures say 'You're like a mist!'

But now we find (verse 15) how we should be approaching this matter. Instead of this arrogant, self-sufficient, self-assertive, self-interested life-style, which is the antithesis of a humble dependance on God and an obedience to the demands of God – instead of all those things, what we really ought to be saying is this: 'If it is the Lord's will, we will live and do this or that.'

And if we don't operate on that basis, then we're boasting, and that is incipient rebellion; and that is the essence of sin.

So James says finally, 'If you know that you should humble yourself, but you're going on in your own arrogant way, you're not just creating all kinds of division and tension in your marriage, your family, and your church: to put it quite bluntly – you're sinning. Because if you know the way to go, and won't do it, that's rebellion.'

Promise, Prayer and Problem People (5: 1–20)

Now, chapter 5. I want to suggest to you that what this chapter is about is promise, prayer and problem people. And it's a short chapter, so we've plenty of time!

The promise
The promise, of course, is identified in verse 7: the Lord is coming again.

One of the great things about Christians is that they have an end in view; they believe that history is not just repeating itself meaninglessly. They know that history is not cyclical, nor is it a chance collision of circumstances. They know that history is the unfolding of the divine purpose, and that God is working inevitably, relentlessly, inexorably, towards the consummation of His eternal will.

And part of all that is the promise that at the appropriate time Christ will return. That is the hope of our calling;
that is what we're working towards, and in the light of
that, we live. We live on earth as men and women with
God in mind; we march through time with eternity in
mind.

Of course, the promise has ramifications.

Prosperity

In the light of the promised return, we need to have some
concerns about prosperity. Now James is really getting
after us again! He's talking about humility, our tongues,
all those silly squabbles in churches, messy marriages and
bad relationships – and now he's going to talk about our
cheque-books!

Well, verses 1–6 are James's diatribe against prosperity. It is not sinful to be wealthy. God owns the cattle
on a thousand hills; Abraham was very wealthy indeed;
Jacob became very wealthy indeed; Jesus was buried in
the tomb of a very wealthy man. Prosperity in and of itself
is not sinful. But there are three things we should bear in
mind and which James addresses: firstly, the means that
we use to gain prosperity may be sinful; secondly, the
attitudes that prosperity produces may well be sinful; and
thirdly, the way we utilise our prosperity may be sinful.

And what he requires is that we evaluate the use of our
prosperity. There is an Eastern European joke that goes,
'Under Capitalism man exploits man; under Communism
it's the other way round!' And of the 2.1 million deaths in
the United States of America last year, 1.5 million were
directly related to diet abuse. While major segments of
our world are dying because of malnutrition, in the Western democracies people are dying because of extravagant
indulgence – too much fat, too much salt, too much
alcohol.

That's what James is talking about here. He's talking about extravagance, about indulgence, about selfishness, about the sin that comes through prosperity.

Prayer

James has something very definite to say about prayer (verse 13). The word 'trouble' there is identical with the word 'suffering' in verse 10, which relates to the theme that he began with: *peirasmois*, trials that can degenerate into temptation if we don't handle them properly.

Verses 13–14 cover a subject that we could spend a lot of time on, but I don't want to omit it. James says (verse 16) that prayer is a dynamic force. To use a colloquial expression, 'Prayer packs a punch!'

Notice who the people are who should pray: those who are in trouble, those who are happy, and those who are sick. For all those, prayer is appropriate. I think that covers just about all of us!

Then James talks specifically about prayer concern for those who are sick. And you will see the same two factors as before: obedience and faith. The obedience factor is this (there are some more imperatives here): 'Let him sing songs of praise. Let him pray. Call for the elders.' Those are commands to be obeyed. But notice that when the elders are called to pray over the person who is sick, it is the prayer offered in faith that makes the sick person well. So you have the obedience factor and you have the faith factor as well.

Let me now address the idea of the prayer of faith that is going to result in sick people being made well. What is the faith spoken of here? That is the crucial question.

Well, faith can be *expectancy*. And there are certain people who say that the prayer of faith means that you just expect God to do it. One aspect of this thinking would be the 'name-it-and-claim-it' approach. That's one interpretation of faith.

Faith, however, can also be *belief*. In other words, when I say that I have faith, I believe something to be true. And there are some people who would say that God at special times, as He works through the elders of the church, will inspire in them a sense of discernment so that they really discern what God's will is in the matter. And with a tremendous sense of belief that this is what God is saying, they pray with great anticipation and conviction that this will happen.

Some, such as John Wimber, speak of the 'word of knowledge'. They describe this as being an inner impression which God gives, and which they then act upon. Those who have reservations about this approach would say, 'How do you *know* that God has given this inner impression?'

The third approach is that faith is *rest and trust*, and that it is *prayer to the Lord*. 'Lord' means 'Sovereign', and so you pray in absolute rest and absolute trust in a sovereign Lord, that He – knowing the end from the beginning and what is best – will make this sick person well and raise him up.

A word of testimony at this point. I would have to say that there have been many, many occasions when I, along with my brother-elders in our church have prayed over the sick and anointed them with oil (and much could be said about James's term 'anointing'[3]). As we have gone in faith, and prayed, and asked God to work through the laying-on of hands – though we do not always even lay on hands – and as we have gathered together and sought God's face, God has always raised people up. Always.

That does not mean that they've been physically healed every time; they haven't. But everyone has testified to a tremendous spiritual uplift; everyone has testified to a tremendous emotional release; and not a few have testi-fied to the fact that God has wonderfully healed them physically. And remember: everybody who is healed, subsequently goes to glory. So keep it in perspective!

Finally, verse 19. Another way that you can show that your faith is working, is by bringing the wanderers home. And I'll just give you my outline here.

1. We should *wonder as people wander* – why are they wandering?

2. Secondly, we should *worry as people wander*, because you see they're living a life in error and they're in danger of the death of a soul; and they may be heaping up a multitude of sins.

3. And we should *work as they wander*. Though God brings them back, He does have a habit of using people. So 'if one of you should wander from the truth and someone should bring him back' – remember this, that you are engaged in the most wonderful work, which glorifies God and brings blessing and shows that your faith is working.

You're being used by God to turn a sinner from error, you're being used by God to save his soul from death, and you're being used by God to cover a multitude of sins.

Thank you, James! You've been a big help to us.

1. Daniel Yankelovich, *New Rules* (Bantam, 1982). Not currently published in Britain.
2. For the benefit of those of you who are ardent Bible students, I will mention that verse 5 is an extremely difficult verse to interpret. The NIV margin is helpful in giving us some clues. But for most of us it isn't a crucial part of the passage, so I have not discussed it here.
3. For example: there are two words for 'anointing'. One is related to the word for 'Christ', and has a ceremonial connotation; the other is a very mundane word which means 'to massage'. Oddly enough, James uses the second rather than the first word. We believe that this is a direct suggestion to use the medicine available, according to medical science available at the time.

THE ADDRESSES:

NOW WE ARE ALL HERE

by Rev. Stuart Briscoe

Acts 10:33

I would like you to turn in your Bibles to chapter 10 of the book of Acts. My text is a short one; the second sentence in verse 33, which in the New International Version reads as follows: 'Now we are all here in the presence of God, to listen to everything the Lord has commanded you to tell us.'

Outside one of the large cities in the USA they are building a very large bridge. What fascinates everybody about this project is not just its great size, but the fact that nothing goes to it, nothing comes from it, and nothing will go over it. They are building it in the middle of a field adjacent to the main highway.

The problem is that a particular political regime once planned to divert the road; hence the need for a new bridge. But that regime lost power, and its successors decided that the road would not now follow that route. But the contract had been signed, and so the bridge is being completed, even though it will never be used.

Nearby, motorists sit in traffic jams on the old, totally inadequate road. They wind down their windows, and hurl all kinds of insults at the poor men working on this bridge which will never be used. The men put up with it for a while, but eventually they erected a large sign on the bridge: WE DON'T KNOW WHY WE ARE HERE, AND WHAT WE ARE DOING, EITHER.

I have been to a number of meetings which I think could have displayed that sign. I trust this is not the case at this Keswick Convention! But, just in case you are wondering why you are here, in case you are wondering what on earth you are going to be doing, let me speak from this passage of Scripture which I think will be helpful to us. For we are all here in the presence of God to listen to everything that the Lord wants us to hear.

Let me identify three things that we find in this sentence. Let me talk first of all about

The people who were at the meeting

Let me remind you of the story. This was a meeting called by a Roman centurion called Cornelius. He had sent for an apostle called Peter. And the Roman centurion called Cornelius brought along his friends and relatives, and gathered them all in his house. Peter came along with six of his friends. And it was Cornelius who said to Peter, in the words of our text, 'Now, we are all here in the presence of God, to listen to everything the Lord has commanded.'

However, we need to look under the surface, because doing so might help us to understand the significance of the meeting. What kind of people were they?

Well, Cornelius was a representative of a certain kind of person who come to this kind of meeting.

Cornelius: a man on a pilgrimage

He was a man who was on a pilgrimage. And I submit to you that some of us here are on a spiritual pilgrimage. We know it; we know exactly what it is we are here for.

Let me remind you of Cornelius' pilgrimage. We know from Scripture, of course, where he started from. He was a Roman. And as you know, when in Rome you do as the Romans do. So what were they doing in Rome in those days? Cornelius, a citizen of Rome, a proud member of the Roman Empire, was by definition a pagan. He was a soldier. He had been posted in Palestine, a particularly troublesome outpost of the Roman Empire.

While he was there he had become a God-fearer – a technical term in those days. It means that he hadn't exactly become a convert to Judaism, but he was on the fringes. He was very much impressed, and strongly influenced by what he saw in Judaism. So, you see, his pilgrimage was this: he had moved from outright paganism to monotheism, he had come to be somebody who believed in and respected the one true God, as opposed to the thousands of gods in the Roman pantheon.

But, having come to know Jehovah, he was still not satisfied in his spiritual pilgrimage. And he had had a vision from the Lord, that he must send for Peter, so that he could find out more of what the Lord wanted to reveal to him. So you see, at the end of this story, he has moved on again, from being merely monotheistic – believing in one God – to possessing an experience of knowing God in Christ in the unique way that Christians believe is possible.

And I suggest to you, that pilgrimage is one that is vitally needed in the Western world today.

You say, surely you are not suggesting that we in the West are pagans, that we need to be moving to monotheism, to Christianity, are you? Aren't we a Christian society already?

And the answer to that is emphatically, yes; that is exactly what I do mean. The late Dr Francis Schaeffer said many years ago that in the Western democracies we were living in the post-Christian era. I remember being some-what resistant to that idea when I heard it, but I have come to the conclusion that whether or not he was right in those days, two or three decades ago, he is most certainly right today. For if we look at the Western democracies today, the prevailing religious emphasis is not Christian. It is not even monotheistic. It is fundamentally pagan.

We believe in a proliferation of gods in our society. I'm not referring to the major religions, but to the fact that people will idealise all manner of things. And they will totally ignore the God who has revealed Himself in cre-ation, who has revealed Himself in Christ, who has revealed Himself in Scripture. In the Western democracies today you can ask the man in the street the most elementary questions concerning that God, and his knowledge will be abysmal.

It doesn't mean that he does not worship. He worships many things: secular, material, pleasurable things; pagan things. Rome in Cornelius' day was a pleasure-orientated society. Even hungry people managed to get to the Circus Maximus, where crowds of over 150,000 would cram in to see the gladiatorial games. It was a violent society; the more blood-thirsty it was, the more they enjoyed it. And I see a picture here of the pagan, pleasure-dominated society that is beginning to develop in our Western world.

The Romans weren't very philosophical like the Greeks; they were pragmatists. They borrowed the philos-ophical speculations and religious concepts of the Greeks, gave them different names, put them to use, and went on training their armies, and building their roads, viaducts and aqueducts. I sense that our society is becoming increasingly pragmatic. It is perfectly happy to justify any means, so long as the ends are reached. And I see a parallel with the Rome of Cornelius' day.

And yet one thing troubled Rome deeply. There was a pervasive sense of doom, a dreadful sense of impending collapse. Abortion was out of hand. Virtually all the Caesars were practising homosexuals. The Barbarians were at the gates, at the borders; and there were desperate problems over marital breakdown and marital unfaithfulness.

Does any of this sound familiar?

This was the society in which Cornelius had been brought up. And it was a society that deeply troubled him. When he finally moved to Palestine and began to observe Judaism, he found many very attractive things in it.

One of the things that he saw, was that the Jews had a tremendous sense of commitment to their beliefs. They were people whom all the might of Rome could not subdue. Rome was going soft at the centre; it was only a matter of time before the Barbarians would be able to overthrow it. But Cornelius saw that the Jews believed in something. They were absolutely committed, and there was something wonderfully attractive about them. There was a morality, a commitment about them. They seemed to be impregnable and almost incorruptible. And he was strangely drawn towards them.

There is all the difference in the world between Rome and Judaism. Our society is busy making gods in man's image, but the truth is that God made man in His own image. That is the pilgrimage that is happening within Cornelius. He sees the possibilities that Rome might fall, and in marked contrast, he sees some people who seem to know where they are going.

He hears that the root of it all is the great God, Jehovah. He moves from the materialism of the empire, to a sense of the spirituality of the King. He becomes a God-fearer.

His pilgrimage is well under way, but he is not through yet, for having come from paganism to monotheism, he still senses that there is more to know. He hungers to *know* more fully this God to whom he is being introduced.

And so with a deep sense of expectancy he sends for Peter, gathers his friends, and says to Peter, 'Now we are all here in the presence of God to listen to everything that the Lord has to say to us.'

I suspect that there are younger people here who haven't come from traditional Christian homes. And you sense that you have been brought up in a pagan society, as I have described it, and you have begun to discover something of who God is. And you are attracted by the prospect of there being some absolutes, as opposed to relativism. You long for something more than the materialism and secularism. You have begun to discover that there is a God, that He is real, and you are hungry to know more. You are on a pilgrimage, and that's why you are here.

If you are like Cornelius, listen as hard as you can to all that the Lord would say to you, through His word, through His people, through His creation; and obey Him, and believe Him, and you will go away blessed.

Peter: a man with problems
Peter is the other key figure in that meeting. Now, I know that he is an apostle, and I know that he is a preacher, but preachers are allowed to have problems too. And Peter is a man with problems. Let me identify four major problems that Peter had.

1. A pressing prayer problem
He had been with the disciples who had observed the Lord Jesus praying. He had listened to Jesus teaching them on the subject of prayer. So he had had a wonderful model and he had wonderful teaching, and he knew that the Master had said, 'Men ought always to pray.' He also

knew that the Master had said, 'When you pray,' not, 'If you pray'.

He believed in prayer and practised it regularly. You remember once that Peter and John were going up to the temple in Jerusalem at 'the hour of prayer' when they met the lame man. He practised prayer spontaneously; when he tried to walk on the water, he began to sink and he began to pray – 'Help!' – a very appropriate prayer.

Peter believed in prayer. In Acts 9, he was suddenly confronted with the death of Dorcas. What did he do? He got on his knees and prayed. He believed in it, and he did it.

He only had one problem with prayer. He had a terrible tendency to go to sleep in prayer meetings! He was praying on the rooftop of one Simon the Tanner. It was a tannery – imagine what it smelt like! But Peter could go up there to pray and manage to fall asleep. He was locked in prison one night, and they were going to behead him the next day; he fell asleep, he couldn't even stay awake to pray then. In the Garden of Gethsemane the Lord told him to stay awake; he fell asleep.

I'm telling you, he had a pressing prayer problem.

Now, we all believe in prayer, don't we? We all do it occasionally! But the problem is that when it really comes down to it, we sometimes wonder what it's all about, and whether it does any good.

We have had a drought in the USA for three months. The only news we've heard so far in the English newspapers is that they have had the Indians out doing their rain dances. But the farmers are praying. They're not sure if it will work or not. They believe in it, and they're doing it, but they aren't sure at all whether it will do any good.

It could be that for some of you at this Convention, that's your problem. Like Peter, you have a pressing prayer problem.

2. A pressing personality problem

There were two main problems in Peter's personality: impetuosity, and inconsistency.

Peter was impetuous. If something needed doing, or even if it didn't need doing, he would do it. He had a sword in the Garden of Gethsemane. Do you think he was really the sort of person who wanted to cut off people's ears? The soldier just ducked. What Peter meant to do was split him right down the middle! It would have started the most dreadful brawl. But Peter didn't think. His motto was 'Ready, shoot, aim'.

It worked fine at times; but the trouble was that Peter's Christianity, like yours and mine, sometimes had to be lived in terms of his personality; and sometimes one's personality can poison one's Christianity.

Peter had a problem of inconsistency, too. For example, the Lord said to him, 'Now, Peter; I want you to go and talk to that Gentile.' But Peter answered defensively: 'But, he eats pigs! Remember what Your book says.' Well, yes; but the same book says that you should have nothing to do with dead bodies. And what was Simon the Tanner's trade? Stripping the hide off dead bodies. And while Peter was lecturing the Lord he was also living in the house of somebody who earned his living from dead bodies.

Peter says one thing, but means another. He sorted himself out on that particular Gentile issue, but you remember what Paul had to say to him in Galatians? After Peter had said all those wonderful things about God having no favourites – we are all one in Christ Jesus, and so on – he refused to eat with Gentiles again, and Paul had to take him out and confront him.

Well, that's Peter! And I think we may well have some people with us at the Convention who not only have a pressing prayer problem, but a pressing personality problem as well.

Let me give you some advice. Listen to all that the Lord has to say to you, listen hard. And respond.

3. A pressing principle problem

Peter was always acting on principle. The Lord Jesus said 'Now, I'm going to wash your feet, Peter.' It was a servant's or women's job in those days (they didn't differentiate between the two).

Maybe it was the slave's night off, and the woman had been liberated – in effect, they'd said 'Wash your own feet!'. Whatever the reason, nobody was washing anybody's feet that night. The youngest disciple should have done it, but the youngest disciple was arguing about who was the youngest disciple. So Jesus said, 'OK, I'll wash their feet.'

He got everything ready, and came to Peter. And Peter – on principle – said, 'You will never wash my feet, never!' The Lord replied, 'If you don't let me do this, then you have no part in me.' And Peter said, 'Well, all right.' So much for principle!

It was the same when the Lord let down the enormous sheet and showed him all the animals, saying 'Don't call unclean what I have called clean.' What was Peter's response? 'Surely not, Lord! I would never do anything like that. It's a matter of principle.'

And yet, a few minutes later, he was talking with the men he had rejected. There are some people who are terribly principled – when it suits them. Have you ever noticed that?

The people on the periphery

We have people on a pilgrimage in this meeting, and we have people with a problem, and there's also a third group of people in this meeting here. That is, the friends and relatives of Cornelius, trying to figure out how on earth they got there. 'Why are we here?' 'I don't know.' 'How did you get here?' 'I don't know.' They were people on the periphery.

At every Keswick convention, people wander into the tent, unsure how they got there. They thought it was a circus. And of course, we have relatives here as well. Some of you have been dragged here by the family, haven't you? And some of you were brought here by friends. And you're wondering why you're here.

Dear periphery people, dear on-the-edges people – just hang in there! Yes, there are some old-timers here who have been on the spiritual pilgrimage a long time. You'll recognise them. And there are problem people here as well. A friend of mine used to say, 'God must love weird people, he sure made plenty.'

There are lots of strange people at Keswick! So, my dear periphery people, do what we have suggested the other people should do. Listen hard to what the Lord is saying to you. That's why we're here.

The purpose for which the meeting was held

Why were those people at the meeting in Acts 10?

There is a stated objective
'We are all here in the presence of God to listen to everything the Lord has commanded you to tell us.'

We have to be careful here. There is a difference between listening and listening. One kind of listening is when somebody has listened as much as he is capable of. So he 'switches off' – but he still nods his head, wisely. 'Yes, yes . . . ' he says, but you know that inside, he has switched off.

Have you noticed in the letters to the seven churches in Revelation, it says: 'He who has ears to hear, let him hear?' Well, you do have two ears. But what is meant is the inner ear, which is going to listen and take seriously what is really going on.

If it is true that God still speaks to people, isn't He worth a listen? That careful, inner-ear attention? That hunger and desire to know the truth? That's why we're here. That's the stated purpose.

There is an implied purpose

'We are all here in the presence of God to listen to everything the Lord has commanded you *to tell us*.' If the preacher senses that the Lord has commanded him to preach in His name, from His word, is it not a reasonable assumption that He will command His people to obey as He has commanded His speaker to speak?

So the purpose is clearly stated; we are here to listen. But the purpose is also very strongly implied; we are here to obey, we are here to do something. And I think it is a reasonable assumption that if we go through a whole week of Convention here, and give God the chance to speak to us, and if we listen with ears that really hear, there will be at least one thing for every single person to do that will require obedience. It would be very strange if that were not the case.

But also,

There is an assumed purpose

The assumption is that 'we are here to experience in some newer, and fuller, and fresher, richer way something more of God'. The only people who are exempt from this possibility are those who have exhausted the resources of God, and know experimentally and experientially all there is to know of Him. So the purpose is quite straightforward. It is clearly stated, strongly implied, and clearly assumed.

The results of the meeting

There are four things here; I will simply outline them for you.

The first result was

A clearer grasp of the gospel

I'm not talking about the elementary basics of the gospel, I'm talking about the full grandeur of the truth of God revealed in Christ from eternity to eternity. And how can we tell that these people who were gathered in the presence of God went away from the meeting with a clearer grasp of the gospel than they had ever had before? We look for something new, there has to be something fresh.

I think back to the years I used to come to Keswick. I could quote you things I learned here from Tom Rees. I could quote from Dr Paul Rees, too, who is over 88 years of age. Last time I was at Keswick Dr Donald English was giving the Bible readings, and I can tell you exactly the things that God taught me through him.

I want to tell you something. If you sit in the presence of God, and you listen with all your ears and with all your heart, and you expect God to tell you something – He can't miss, and you can't miss. You cannot but go away with a clearer grasp of the gospel.

A deeper experience of the Spirit

While Peter was speaking, the Holy Spirit came on all who heard the message, and the circumcised believers who had come with him were astonished that the gift of the Holy Spirit had been poured out even on the Gentiles. For they heard them speaking in tongues and praising God.

How did they go away from that meeting? With a clearer grasp of the gospel and a deeper experience of the Spirit. The Spirit of God has so much work to do in our lives! Purging, transforming, deepening – that's what will happen.

A broader vision of the divine will
The circumcised believers who had come with Peter were astonished that the gift of the Holy Spirit had been poured out on the Gentiles. They began to see something utterly incredible, for the first times in their lives; that God actually loved the Gentiles too. Why they hadn't seen that I don't know, because it permeates the Old Testament, but they hadn't got the message.

But they suddenly began to realise that the lamb of God slain before the foundation of the world had shed His blood for both Jew and Gentile. And that whosoever will, may come. And that God has no favourites. What a need there is today for the Church of Jesus Christ to have a better sort of vision of the divine will!

A fuller understanding of the Church's mandate
The Church would have gone on rather nicely without too many problems, while they just had Jews in it. Thank God, Jesus, who had given the keys to Peter, said, 'Now, unlock the door to the Gentiles,' and as soon as he did, they began to discover the wonder and the immensity and the glory of what the Church was intended to be.

The Church was intended to be the means of transcending barriers, instead of erecting them. It was intended to be the means of building bridges over every schism, crack and fragmentation in human society. Yet the Church of Jesus Christ is on the wane, the Church of Jesus Christ is on the defensive, the Church of Jesus Christ is slipping into irrelevance in many parts of the Western world today.

Now, I'll tell you something: if you gather here in the presence of God this week, to listen to everything that God has to say to you, you can't possibly go away without a keener sense of the Church's mandate.

Those people building that bridge really didn't know why they were there, and they really didn't know what they were doing; but you know why you are here, don't you? And you know what you're going to do, don't you? You are going to gather in the presence of God to listen to everything that God has commanded to tell you.

THE FEAR OF THE LORD

by Canon Keith Weston

Philippians 2:12–13

It was with a little bit of turmoil in my mind that I came to Keswick with my notes all written out. It's quite a responsibility to be standing here! And I think part of my apprehension was that I knew that God was saying this message for me personally; and who was I to stand up here and say it to all you people?

And then Stuart Briscoe on that first night[1] quoted, you remember, that passage from Acts where Cornelius said to Peter, 'We're all here, in the sight of God, to hear all that you have been commanded by the Lord' – and you can imagine what effect that had on me! So I pray that what is said now may be from the Lord, as commanded by Him, and in no sense from me personally, because I sit under the Word as you do, and I believe that God wants to speak to all of us very seriously tonight.

'With fear and trembling'

Please turn with me to Philippians 2:12–13. These are very familiar verses, and I expect that many ministers here tonight who have the duty of preaching have preached, as I have, on the lovely ideas in those two verses: that there

is a perfect balance between our obligation to work out
what Christ has done for us on the cross in the finished
work of Calvary, and the fact that it has to be worked out
in our own experience. And we balance it in our preaching, as Paul does here, by the equal and opposite statement – and what a joy it is to add it – that 'God is at work
in you, both to will and to work for his good pleasure.'

I have often preached on those two verses. But what
struck me as being the thought for tonight is those little
words which have such significance between those two
'equal and opposites', which I confess that I've never
preached on before, and which have a significance which I
find, when I look at it and meditate on it and pray over it
to be quite, quite alarming. 'Work out your own salvation'
says Paul, 'with fear and trembling.'

And I ask myself, where and how does that fit in my
Christian experience? Why does the apostle add those
words 'with fear and with trembling'? One might be
tempted to say, surely there is no place for fear and
trembling in the life of the spiritually-minded man or
woman. And all one's remembered verses come tumbling
into one's mind.

For example 1 John 4:18 says: 'Perfect love casts out
fear . . . He who fears is not perfected in love.' Yet here is
the Apostle saying, 'Work out your salvation with fear
and trembling.' And I ask again, how do those two equal
and opposite head-on-in-collision thoughts of Scripture
really fit in my personal experience? When have I ever
trembled as a Christian in working out my own salvation?

Or, again, as Paul writes to Timothy, that young man
who was I think prone to fear and feeling ashamed of the
gospel: 'God did not give us' he says to Timothy 'a spirit of
timidity but a spirit of power and love and self-control'
(2 Tim. 1:7). We're pretty good these days about talking
about power in the Church; we're not so bad about talking

about love, and sometimes we do actually get around to talking about self-control. And we love the idea that fear has no place in the Christian life, least of all when we look up into the face of our heavenly Father. What does Paul mean – 'Work out your own salvation with fear and trembling'? How is it that he can tell his Philippian friends that?

Oh, you may say, it's simply a matter, surely, of the words that he's using, and you're misunderstanding the words. Well, it's true that we do have to be careful about these words to get the exact meaning, but as I looked them up I found that it's even more perplexing. When Paul writes to Timothy, 'timidity' is a far weaker word, a fairly innocuous word. That was Timothy's problem; he was a little bit scared of standing up as a Christian. And we can understand that – it's a far easier word in Greek; it's not the word used in Philippians.

When you examine the word there, you find not a weak word but a very, very strong one. Indeed, in one place in the old version, it's called 'terror', and that's its meaning in classical Greek. It's the sort of thing, says the Classical Greek lexicon, that actually turns armies to flight.

And where, I ask, does that fit in my Christian experience? Because I don't think I've ever felt quite like that.

No wonder, then, it's accompanied by the word 'trembling'. Paul links the words like that three times in three separate places. And I throw the question out to you: has that ever had any place in your Christian life, where your heavenly Father is concerned?

I don't think we know much about this. But when you come to think of it, as I've been doing over these last months, the Bible is full of this teaching. And I find that I've 'conveniently' passed over it, or paraphrased it to mean something a little less.

We read of people in the New Testament who were walking in the fear of God, and it runs off the tongue so easily, doesn't it – and all we mean is that they were rather good, godly folk. Well, I'm quite sure they were. But is it just a folk statement that has been handed down until it comes to mean nothing more than that – that they walked in the fear of God? There are forty-five places in the New Testament where this Greek word occurs, and the vast majority speak of our proper attitude to God, and it's very difficult to step around that.

Indeed, it says in the Psalms, though I have no idea whether there's a corollary between the Old Testament Hebrew and the New Testament Greek, that 'the fear of the Lord is the beginning of wisdom'. And we've preached on it, and we've quoted it; and all we mean by it usually is 'Oh yes, pay God respect and reverence.'

I don't see that. As you put these verses together one after another, their cumulative effect is precisely what they say: that the first lesson in godliness is to have a profound *fear of the Lord*.

The fear of the Lord

We stroll into the tent and we say, 'What's this new speaker going to do? Alistair Begg – we've not heard him before,' and we award him points for his performance – when what God is expecting of us is to sit under the Word, and to know the terror of those who sit under the Word of God when it's applied like a dart straight to your heart. The Gehazi syndrome is not a nice idea, but it's a sin that lurks in this tent tonight. I'm sure of it.

It may be objected: *You're over-stating it, aren't you? We're not supposed to be afraid of God! It simply means to reverence God and His things, surely*.

And yes, I'm sure that's included; that's one of the outworkings of this word. But even that quality is in short supply today. It grieves us all to hear the way God's name is taken in vain, even in Christian circles, and the way God's things are made a source of ridicule, even in the kind of jokes we tell each other in Christian circles. We're often so familiar with God that we know nothing of what it is to put off your shoes from off our feet because the place we're treading on is holy ground.

Okay, that's cultural, isn't it? Moses understood what was meant by that; it was just cultural. Muslims to this day put their shoes off. So do the Japanese when they enter their 'houses of God'. But it's not our custom so it doesn't mean anything to us.

But how do you do the hermeneutics, as the theologians say, and bring that into our experience? What is it that God would say to us who come into a marquee like this?

'Hold it! Think where you're coming.'

You're coming into a holy place where God intends that business should be done with Him, and that you should not be allowed to go out the same way as you came in.

Indeed, the prayer that I think needs to be said more than any other prayer these days is, 'Oh God, have mercy upon me!' And you know, there won't be revival in this country until that's the prayer that comes wrung from people's hearts. We talk about revival, but what we talk about is jolly hand-clapping and chorus singing. I don't see that in Scripture. I see revival beginning when the tears break forth from your eyes, and you cry – and you mean it – 'Oh God, have mercy on me, the sinner!'

That's how the man spoke in Jesus' parable – 'the sinner'. Not 'those sinners' but 'me, the sinner'.

'I'm the only one in the tent tonight. Oh God, have mercy upon me. I'm terrified at what I see in my own heart, as I stand in your presence in all your holiness and glory before me.'

We sing 'Holy, holy, holy', yet somehow the words are so familiar that they roll off our tongues and it doesn't make any impact on us. And I believe the Holy Spirit tonight would bring us up sharp, myself included, until perhaps we do indeed cry, 'Oh God, have mercy upon me.'

What would it be if this place were shaken as the doors of the Temple were when God appeared before Isaiah there in Isaiah 6? If you had seen God in all His holiness, would you have cried out like Isaiah did? Of course you would! There would be fear and trembling, and that is the beginning of wisdom.

I believe Philippians 2:12 means precisely what it says. It's as though God is saying to us through it, 'Man or woman, do you profess to be a Christian? Work out your salvation, won for you at such tremendous cost in all its totality and finality in the work of Jesus Christ upon the cross for you; work that out, and what it means in your life, not in that careless, petty, thoughtless way that has characterised your life these past months and years (God have mercy upon you!); not even in that carefree happy-go-lucky sort of way that sees the Christian life as all fun and frolic – but with fear and trembling.'

Why? He answers his own question.

God is at work in you

'Because it is God who is at work in you both to will and to work for His good pleasure' (verse 13). Don't lose the impact of it. Take care! It runs off the tongue, you know it so well. But do you get the feel of what he's saying in this verse? It's not just a comforting thought to match the responsibility of verse 12. It's not a balancing, compensating statement at all. *It's the explanation.* You and I can only work out our own salvation with fear and trembling, *because* it is God who is at work in you.

This is an immensely sobering, breath-taking thought. God actually cares about the standard of your spiritual life. He is committed to working in you.

'How dare you adopt such a careless attitude in your Christian life! Have you not realised that it is God, no less, God who is at work in you?' Oh, doesn't that challenge your triviality! Doesn't that just kill off all your truculent self-confidence!

Listen: God is at work in you, to will and to work what He pleases. And again, that absolutely reduces us in size, until we're grovelling. So often we think, it's all about what pleases us, what *we* want. There's not a word of that here. It's all about what He wants and what pleases Him.

When you think about it, it's something to make you stop in your tracks, to send a sudden shudder down your spine. God is at this moment, in this meeting, at work in us who love Him, and seek to serve Him (but oh, how pathetically); God is at work in us.

Because what He wants to see is not, may I say it, some blessing in your life, but what pleases Him. It may not look much of a blessing to you. Oh, it will be a blessing, I know, but it may involve hardship, it may involve all kinds of things that your heart rebels against, and says, 'No, not that, Lord.' But is that going to stop God working? Knowing the very fear and trembling with which we ponder the thought, the possibility that God could be interested in our pathetic little lives? That He, the Lord God of heaven, is at work in us now, to work out in us what He pleases?

That is an astonishing truth, and that, Paul says, is the reason why you work out your own salvation with fear and trembling. Your life is in the hands of the living God. He is the potter, and we are the clay. And who are we to answer God and say, 'I don't want to be made that way, you can't have it like that'?

God is sovereign and, whether you like it or not, He is at work in you, to do and to will what is His good pleasure, and not what suits your susceptibility.

I know I am quoting out of context, but it seems so appropriate to quote Hebrews 10:31, where we are told that 'it is a fearful thing to fall into the hands of the living God'. We say in our testimonies, 'When I was such-and-such an age, I gave my heart to the Lord Jesus Christ' – no you didn't! You fell into the hands of the living God, like a lump of clay.

'I gave my heart to God' . . . 'I surrendered my life to Him' . . . they run off the tongue, those phrases, don't they? But if you did, then God is at work in you, and He is not going to be put off, He is at work in your life tonight. How dare you adopt a trivial attitude to the responsibility of working out what that means in life!

Trivialising God

I am ashamed how so often in my own life I trivialise sin. I am ashamed of the way I often dream of going against the will of God, and of how easily the seed thought is planted in the mind. And I ask myself, how dare I dream of rebelling against Him when He convicts me of sin, and goes on convicting me of sins, which I hug onto and rather enjoy! How dare I refuse to listen to Him, and think I can push Him to one side! How dare I self-centredly face the future, as if it were up to me where I am going to go, or where I should be at this point!

How easily, how trivially, I can make decisions, as if God were *not* working in me to will and to do His good pleasure instead of my good pleasure. And I may, for all I know, be aiming in totally the wrong direction, because I simply haven't dared to take seriously the thought that I am not my own, I have been bought with a price. God is at work in me, not me at work on God to make Him agree with what I want to do. How dare we self-centredly live our lives as if He were!

So often we treat God as if He is there to accede to every demand and project and pleasure. But that's not the way it is spoken here, is it? In sovereign authority, it is His to see that we do His will, and He's jolly well going to make sure that we do His will. Whether we come kicking and squealing His way, or (as it says here) in fear and trembling, He will bring us there. I think the Bible has the right word here. It is a frightening thought.

What did the thief say to the other thief, railing and cursing on that first Good Friday, Jesus crucified between them? He said what he should have said: 'Dost thou not fear God?' You go off to your daily work, and you go along with the sins of our society, and you brush your hands and say that you can do nothing about it. Dost thou not fear God?

You accept standards in your life for what you watch on television, or the books you read, and it is all absorbed into your mind. Dost thou not fear God? You have got to answer to Him.

Of course, it's the attitude of this godless world in which we live – read Romans 3:18. Does it not make you tremble when you read in the papers of some person who has died after a lifetime of publicly ridiculing God or His law, or the things of God? Some politician, some corrupt businessman, some popular comedian who's made thousands laugh by ridiculing the things of God? Doesn't it make you tremble when you hear that they have died, and have passed into the holy presence of the Judge of all mankind? It says in Scripture, every idle thought, every idle word will be judged. God have mercy upon me.

What the courts here below either fail to catch up with, or are not concerned about now, they will have to answer before the Supreme Court of the living God. There is nothing covered that will not be revealed, nothing hidden that will not be known. Those are most uncomfortable verses in Scripture, aren't they?

I think this is one of the chief reasons why Paul was so
earnest in his evangelism. 'Knowing the terror of the
Lord' it says in the old version, 'we persuade men and
women . . .' (2 Cor. 5:11). But what about us, then, who
in the mercy of God have been saved, persuaded,
redeemed, and brought to know Jesus Christ? Is there no
place for soberness on this matter in our hearts – a true,
holy fear that marks our lives, so that as Peter says, we
'conduct ourselves with fear' (1 Pet. 1:17)?

Beware the trivial sins

I've been reading John Bunyan's *Pilgrim's Progress*, and
at this point in my preparation I came across that passage
which I remember losing sleep over in childhood. It's that
passage where Christian, in the Interpreter's House,
encounters a man in an iron cage.

'How camest thou in this condition?'

'I left off to watch and be sober; I laid the reins upon
the neck of my lusts; and sinned against the light of the
world, and the goodness of God: I grieved the Spirit
and he is gone; I tempted the devil, and he has come to
me; I have provoked God to anger, and he has left me;
I have so hardened my heart, that I cannot repent . . .'

Then said Christian, 'Is there no hope but you must
be kept in this iron cage of despair?'

'No, none at all.'

'Why? The Son of the Blessed is very pitiful.'

'I have crucified him to myself afresh, I have despised
his person, I have despised his righteousness, I have
counted his blood an unholy thing, I have done despite
to the spirit of grace: therefore I have shut myself out of
all the promises; and there now remains to me nothing
but threatenings, dreadful threatenings, fearful threatenings of certain judgement and fiery indignation,

which shall devour me as an adversary . . . God hath
denied me repentance, his word gives me no encouragement to believe; Yea, himself hath shut me up in
this iron cage: nor can all the men in the world let me
out. O eternity! eternity! how shall I grapple with the
misery that I must meet with in eternity?'

It's hard-hitting stuff, isn't it? Part of me wishes that that
thought was not in the Scriptures, but you notice how he is
quoting Hebrews 6:3–6 and 10:26–28? There it speaks of
the person who has spurned the Son of God and profaned
the blood of the Covenant by which he was sanctified, and
outraged the Spirit of God. 'It is a fearful thing to fall into
the hands of the living God.'

Paul wrote to those Corinthians, of whom we are hearing in the morning Bible readings, 'I tremble lest the
serpent deceive you by his cunning. Your thoughts will be
led astray from a sincere and pure devotion to Christ' (Cf.
2 Cor. 11:3).

'Work out your own salvation', says the apostle, 'with
fear and trembling' – fear of the awful corrupting corro-
sive influences of those little sins that you and I think so
little about, and which God may be putting His finger on
tonight in this tent. I believe He wants to because He
loves you. He wants you to be rid of those sins, before you
come to that point.

'Let this be a warning to you,' said Interpreter to Christian before he went on his way. Beware of trivial sins, for
no sin is trivial. 'Work out your own salvation in fear and
trembling', yes, in fear and trembling, lest you be bound
to be spurning the love of the God who sent His only
begotten Son, because He loved you so much; He gave
Him on the cross to die for your eternal salvation.

How dare you think that sin is trivial! How dare you!
Dost not thou fear God?

I remember when I was a curate starting out in the ministry being reassured by my vicar when I did not know how to counsel a dear elderly Christian who had become greatly troubled that she might have committed the unforgivable sin. 'Keith,' he said, 'if Mary had committed the unforgivable sin, she would not be troubled in the least. The fact that she is troubled at all, is the surest sign of the working of the grace of God in her heart.'

If God has troubled us during this address, if He has found us out, then the Scripture says, 'Today, if you hear his word, harden not your hearts.'

Repentance is the biblical fruit of godly sorrow. You could say that there can be no true repentance until there has been that godly sorrow which may be accompanied by fear and trembling.

It means an honest facing up to every sin which God in His love reveals to us lurking in our lives. It means a God-given grace to turn from that sin and have done with it. It may, and probably will, involve some very hard and very practical action. Whoever suggested that confession was easy? Repentance is not cheap, and neither is grace. Repentance which is God-given is costly, a total change of mind leading to a total change of life-style.

May I encourage you as I close?

Listen to the words of David – David, of all people! – when he sinned very grievously before God. He committed adultery with Bath-Sheba. I believe that Psalm 32 belongs to that period, after that ghastly, appalling sin which he tried to brush out of his mind, as it says, but couldn't. That Psalm begins, as you all well know, 'Blessed is the man whose sins are forgiven, whose wrongs are pardoned. Happy is the man whom the Lord no longer accuses of doing wrong, who is freed from all deceit' (verses 1–2).

Has God spoken to you tonight? Has God spoken to me tonight? You know, you can't rush out after a Monday meeting like this, without surely remaining quiet and searching your hearts before you go to bed tonight; without saying, on your knees before God, 'Search me, O God, and try my heart, and see if there be any wicked way in me, and lead me in the way everlasting.' And we may add to the Psalmist's words, 'No matter, Lord, what it costs, for I fear and tremble at the consequences of allowing sin to harbour in my heart.'

We've mentioned Gehazi. May I just tell you that Gehazi returns to the pages of the Old Testament, three chapters after his sin. I can only assume that he was restored and pardoned and the servant of Elisha once again.

Do you want to be restored? Perhaps tonight your path will be away from the dark paths of sin, via the cross, back to God.

1. This address is included in the present volume, p.148.

ONE WITH JESUS

by Rev. David Jackman

Romans 6:1–5

Last night we ended our meeting with that searching question, 'Dost thou not fear God?' And in our Bible reading
this morning, we were reminded that this God exercises
His sovereignty in suffering, dying love which we see as
we come to that cross about which we have just been
singing. And it's in that sequence of biblical teaching that
I invite you to turn with me tonight to the letter to the
Romans, chapter 6 and the first 14 verses.

In this central section in Romans – indeed, all the way
through the letter – Paul is expounding the gospel, and
what it means to live as a Christian. Chapter 5 of Romans
has been all about Christ's death on our behalf, for us.
The whole idea of that chapter is that the Lord Jesus
Christ did for us what we could not do, as Paul explains,
for example, in that famous verse 5:6.

And through what He did through His death on the
cross, we are brought within the sphere of God's free
grace, which means that we are forgiven and accepted in
Christ, as in verse 18 at the end of the chapter 5.

So Romans 5 is about that great biblical doctrine of
justification by faith; that Jesus Christ died for us and
apart from us, that He has carried the punishment for our

sin, and in His death He has purchased our forgiveness, and opened the kingdom of heaven for all believers. And we love to repeat that chapter and say to one another, 'We can contribute nothing at all towards that salvation. It is the free gift of God's grace.'

But when you come into chapter 6, there is a sudden shift, because there at the beginning of verse 2 Paul says, 'We died.' So we have moved from looking at the status we have with God as the result of the death of the Lord Jesus, to looking at a moral obligation that we have before God as a result of our death. We died to sin.

'But,' you say, 'Jesus died on a cross outside Jerusalem on a Friday afternoon 1,950 years ago, and here am I alive tonight in Keswick. I haven't died!'

'Wrong!' says Paul, in verse 3. 'Don't you know that you have?' Look at how many times he stresses that: verse 2, we died to sin; verse 4, we were buried with Him through baptism into death; verse 5, we have been united with Him in His death; verse 6, our old self was crucified with Christ; verse 8, we died with Christ.

Have you ever felt as if somebody was trying to tell you something? Don't you *know*, says Paul?

More than that, we have been raised with Him (verse 5). Have you noticed the little preposition that appears again and again in these verses? '*With Christ*'. I want us to think tonight what it means for us to be one with Jesus.

Usually, we associate that phrase 'with Christ' either with those early disciples who were literally with Christ, living and talking with Jesus, and learning from Him during his earthly ministry – in other words, it has to do with the past – or we relate it to our fellow Christians who have died, who have vacated the body and are at a new address which Paul describes in Philippians 1 as being *with Christ*, 'which is far better'. In other words, it has to do with the future.

But we will be quite wrong if we think the New Testament has nothing to say about our *present* association with Christ. In fact, that is the key to making real progress in the business of Christian living.

Let me suggest to you that there are here, some

Facts to be faced (verses 1–4)

Verse 2 is quite unequivocal: We died to sin. How could we go on living in it? Not, 'We should die'; not 'Some day, we will die'; not 'Some super-Christians have managed to die' – but 'we died to sin'.

If you were to say to Paul, 'When did it happen?', his answer would be to point to baptism. He has not forgotten that Christ died at a particular point in history, and that years have elapsed between the crucifixion and the writing of these words to the Christians at Rome. And we must not forget that we move further away from that death in time and in history every second of our lives. So when Paul talks about baptism, he is not talking about some magic link-up with the past. Baptism is essentially an expression of faith and commitment in the present, and despite differing views about the mode of baptism, it is universally accepted among Christians as the initiatory ordinance or sacrament into the body of Christ, into the Christian Church.

We know that all the water can do is to make you wet. Yet it is the outward spiritual sign of the inward, visible grace. And it is by that grace operating in our lives that we are initiated into the benefits and effects of Christ's death and resurrection (verse 4).

There is a helpful parallel in 1 Corinthians 10, where Paul talks about the Jews who came out of Egypt being baptised into Moses in the cloud and in the sea. That new community was created through the mighty exodus event when God by His right arm took His people out of bondage into freedom. Redeemed by the blood of the Passover lamb, and led by the pillar of fire and cloud, the people passed through the sea and came to Mount Sinai. There they received God's covenant instructions for the behaviour of people living in fellowship with Him.

The pattern is exactly the same in the New Testament. Our great exodus was accomplished at the cross, where Jesus triumphed over all the hostile powers of sin that bind us and condemn us to death eternally. And through the blood of our lamb, the Lamb of God who bears away the sin of the world, we have been brought out of darkness into His light. We have been reconstituted as the new covenant people of God, and in His resurrection He has opened the way for us to experience the eternal light of God planted within the soul of man.

When I put my faith in Christ by God's grace (of which baptism is the outward sign) I die to the power of sin. My old way of living of sin and self, says Paul, is buried. I enter into the potential of a new life. I enter the community of redeemed men and women who live in covenant relationship under the lordship of Jesus Christ. The cross of Christ and His glorious resurrection are no longer events in the remote past wholly separate from me. Now my whole life is determined by them. I am a part of their fruit.

There was a real death, a real burial, a real resurrection. They are real events in history, but because they were the actions of the eternal son of God, they have reference backwards and forwards in time. The cross is the demonstration *at* one point in time, but *for* all time, of what God has always been: compassionate and gracious, slow to anger, abounding in steadfast love and faithfulness, maintaining covenant mercy to thousands, and forgiving wickedness, rebellion and sin.

That is our God. By that work of salvation, Abraham was justified, you are justified, and I am justified. Paul says there are facts that we need to face. Jesus has achieved it all. The new order into which he has brought us began back there in history, when the balance of spiritual power was for ever settled. And you and I are beneficiaries of that here and now through faith in Christ, so we are dead to sin, even to death itself.

Logic to be learned (verses 5–10)

Verse 5 reiterates the principle: 'If we have been united with him in his death, we will certainly also be united with him in his resurrection.'

The 'if . . . then' construction is the form of a logical proposition. If this – then that. It doesn't express any doubt, it follows a logical argument. We are one with Jesus, says Paul, both in His death and His resurrection. You can't have one without the other, because the Bible sees a single salvation event.

Paul leads us through the logic of this in two stages. He says, 'I want you to get your mind around this.' It is as we get our minds around the truth of God in Scripture that we are given understanding to apply it in our lives.

So Paul says firstly, we are *united with Him in His death*. He expounds this in verses 6 and 7. Anyone who has died, has been freed from sin. The New English Bible translates this as 'the man we once were has been crucified with Christ.'

Well, what sort of people were we once?

When we became Christians, our lives were controlled and conditioned by sin. Our faculties were under sin's control, we had an appetite for sin. In terms of verse 14, sin was our master. We would not have necessarily have thought of it that way, and we may have had all sorts of sophisticated ways of explaining and masking it; but the plain biblical fact is, that whoever commits sin is the slave of sin.

What has happened now? Well, says Paul, not only did I trust Him as my sin-bearer, who made the full atonement, so that I may justly be pardoned by a holy God; but as I turned to Him in faith, that required me also to turn in repentance. I was turning away from my old way of living, the rebellion that would not let God be God in my life, and because that was the root of all my sinfulness, I consigned that old self to death, with Jesus.

Why? Verse 6: 'So that the body of sin might be rendered powerless', and that I may no longer be its slave. That old self was crucified, in the sense that it was rendered powerless to enslave me any longer. My faculties are the same, but sin is no longer in control. And that new man (verse 7) is a man who having died has been freed from the tyranny of sin.

So the power that we need to live the new life is in Christ's death on the cross. That is where there is power sufficient to render sin powerless in my life. It's not the same thing as saying that we are sinless. Paul is presenting sin as a tyrant master which has enslaved every one of us. He presents it as a hostile power that has invaded and occupied every part of our lives. Our minds, our emotions, our wills, every part of our make-up is infected and occupied by sin the tyrant.

But, says Paul, the death of our Lord Jesus is the great conquest by which sin has been cast down from its throne. When I trusted Him as my Saviour I had a new Lord, a liberator; and we live under His dominion now, so that if he is in charge, sin cannot be.

Do you remember Jesus' own words? 'I tell you the truth, everyone who sins is a slave to sin . . . [but] if the Son sets you free, you will be free indeed' (John 8:34, 36).

When we hear things like that, we think it's too good to be true. But wait – we're not building our faith on our experience are we? Before you begin to say 'That isn't true in *my* life,' let the Bible speak to you. Build your faith on God's Word. What does it say in verse 8? 'If we died with Christ, we believe that we will also live with him.'

The cross and resurrection go together. God proclaimed the sufficiency and acceptability of the death of Jesus on the cross – how? By raising Him from the dead. So He cannot die again (verse 9). He dealt with sin once for all, and the wages of sin and death have been paid by His victory. Death no longer has mastery over the Christian believer.

Death was the inevitable penalty for sin. But Jesus paid that penalty to the full, and (verse 4), through the glory of the Father, Jesus was raised from the dead. So the death He died, He died for sin, once for all, but the life He lived, He lives to God. You see, the resurrection proves that all that is behind Him; He lives today triumphantly as the Lord of lords, and the King of kings.

So for the Christian who is united to Jesus by faith, there is a new life to be lived – the resurrection life, a life in which we find our true selves for the first time, as we begin to become what God has always desired us to be. The image of God, broken by sin through the fall, begins to be restored in the Christian who lives a new life in Christ. That's the logic of the cross and the resurrection.

We need to learn it. You see, it transforms our attitude to the Christian life. And it explains why we can never go beyond the cross. Verse 10 tells us Jesus has died to sin: that was the object of His death. In His dying He did something to the power of death, and therefore to the devil, which meant that he could never hurt, or destroy or touch Him. He put the principalities and powers of that old world order to flight. He sent them underground, he triumphed over them in the cross, and as a result, we who are united to Him by faith, are liberated from the control of the power of that old era, with all its hostility to God, and God's will in our lives, and it is unable to enslave any longer those who live by faith, united to Christ.

Lastly, there are

Deductions to be drawn (verses 11–14)

What does this all mean in practice? Does it mean that we live an exalted life, untroubled by temptation? Does it mean that it is possible for us to be immune from the flesh, the world and the devil?

On the contrary, we find ourselves in the front line under constant attack from the enemy. He is always trying to win back the territory that Christ has liberated. So Paul calls us in these verses to a decision in life here and now, but it can only be made on the basis of having died and been raised with Christ.

That's always the way in the Old Testament, isn't it – the demands of Scripture are based on the teaching. And there are two commands that we have to take seriously.

First God tells us in His Word who we are and what we are, then He tells us what to do on the basis of that, so that when we have faced the facts, and learnt the logic, He says: Now, this is the application. Verse 11: *Count yourselves dead to sin*. Verse 13: *Offer yourselves to God*. These are things that are our responsibility. They are based on what Christ has done, they depend entirely on the dynamic of the cross and the empty tomb, but we have to act on this. We have to recognise the facts, and live on the basis of those facts.

Verse 11 is a fact. 'Count yourselves dead to sin, but alive to God.' Live out that reality. Paul does not say, 'If you can somehow work up enough objective faith to really believe it, it might come true.' No: he is saying, 'Believe it, because it is already so.' Therefore (verse 12) don't let sin reign in your mortal body. Again, he is not saying, 'Sin is in control of you, you must pull yourself together and stop it.' He is saying, 'Christ in His cross and resurrection has destroyed the authority of Satan, and deposed the tyrant's sin. So do not allow him a foothold in your life!'

How do we ensure it? By the positive of verse 13. Instead of going back to that old way of living with its tyranny of failure, says Paul, make all that you are available to God every day. Isn't that what it means to be taking up the cross daily? That we go on daily identifying ourselves with Christ, in His way of sacrificial love? That by faith we commit everything to God's hands? We carry that cross, as anyone going out to his crucifixion did, with no plans of our own for the future, entirely abandoned to the will of God. And we discover, in that which seems to be the end of everything, the beginning of real life, eternal life, in the resurrection power of Christ.

So, Paul says, give your whole being over to God, so that every faculty, every member, can be used as an instrument (the word literally means 'a weapon') for righteousness. Put all your weight on the side of your Liberator by daily dedication, and as you do that by faith, you can take the enormous assurance of verse 14 to yourself.

Jesus is our Lord, so sin can no longer lord it over those who are under the lordship of Christ. And there is this marvellous promise; sin will not regain its dominion over us as we continue to trust in Christ, because we are no longer under the law which binds us under condemnation to the sentence of death. Instead we belong to a new era. We are in Christ, we are with Jesus, one with His death and resurrection. We have entered a new environment. We are under grace.

So the chapter ends, verse 22. Now that you have become slaves to God, the benefits you reap lead to holiness. It's part of becoming more like the Lord Jesus. And the result? Eternal Life, here already, there in its fullness. To live under the rule of grace is to be one with Jesus through faith in Him, and to know increasingly the victory of Christ's cross and His glorious resurrection. Hallelujah, what a Saviour!

FIND OUT WHAT PLEASES THE LORD

by Rev. Alistair Begg

Colossians 1:9–14

Will you please turn with me this evening first of all to
Ephesians 5:8–10, and to that phrase which the NIV
translates like this: 'Find out what pleases the Lord'.

It is that phrase that forms the title and the framework
for the study that we share together now. Paul's great
concern was for the people to whom he wrote to grasp,
and be grasped by, fresh discoveries of Christ's lordship in
their lives. Writing to the church at Ephesus, indeed writing in all of his letters, he treats the matter of the lordship
of Christ, not as an option for some, but as an obligation
for all.

And it is very important that we underline that in our
thinking. When he wrote to the church at Corinth, he said
of himself and his colleagues: 'We make it our goal to
please him' (2 Cor. 5:9). When he wrote to the church at
Thessolonica, he said, 'We instructed you how to live in
order to please God' (1 Thess. 4:1). And it is not just
Pauline references which are replete with this insistence,
that the discovery of the lordship of Christ is a matter for
every believer.

Yet in spite of the fact that Scripture insists on this, it is
customary to hear people refer again and again to the

nature of Christ's lordship in such terminology as people use when making a choice in buying a new car. I am referring to the options which are available on certain cars. You can have the basic version, or you can have the L version, or the GL version, or the X version, or whatever it is; and if you go in and drive these different cars, the salesman will tell you, 'Basically, this version is OK, it will do everything that you need, but it is fun to have all the extras . . .'

And as I move around I meet people who have a notion of the lordship of Jesus Christ directly akin to that. They mistakenly believe that it is possible to adopt some basic version of Christianity and choose not to take on the optional package which will add special dimensions to it.

Thus we find that people think that the discovery of Christ's lordship is perhaps only for those who have become involved in pastoral ministries, or have become missionaries, or have become extra-devoted to Christ, and that those who are the 'normal' Christians are able to stand back and look at those who have gone for the more expanded version.

If I do nothing else in this study, I would like with God's help to explode that mythology that lingers in many of our minds. I believe this notion may be more responsible than any other for the prevalent conviction in the hearts of many, that the task of the ministry is primarily that of the Christian professionals – whether it be missionary service, pastoral ministry, whatever it is; that those who are the Christians in the market-place of life are like those driving on a coach from Glasgow to Carlisle, sitting in the back while the professional drives. And they believe that they have the option to applaud when he drives well, to criticise when he drives badly, and to pass their comments always towards the front, believing that there is a different standard for him or for her than there is for those who sit in the passenger seats.

John Stott's great phrases have lived with me for many years. He said on one occasion,

> Confrontation with Christ is the Christian's zest, and conformity to Christ is the Christian's standard. Which Christian? Every Christian, tinker, tailor, soldier, sailor, rich man, poor man, student, grandfather, grandmother, housewife, bank teller, painter, factory worker, insurance sales man, doctor, nurse, farmer, whoever who are. There is only one standard, to live under the lordship of Jesus Christ. It is not an option. There are no spectators, there is no applause for another, for we must all find out what pleases the Lord.

It would be strange, wouldn't it, to bear allegiance to Jesus Christ, and then live my life disregarding what would please Him. And yet some do, and I believe the reason they do is because they think that lordship is a special package which they have decided not to choose. I say again to you tonight, there is only one package, and it is confrontation with Christ, and it is conformity to Christ.

If we were to list all of the characteristics tonight of a life that pleases God, it would be a very long list, and you would all have left long before I had finished. So I am not going to attempt to do that. Instead, I am going to use the first prayer that Paul prays for the church at Colosse. Remember that our purpose is this: to answer the question, what pleases the Lord?

The discovery that we make of Christ's lordship, incidentally, is not made in a library, it is not made in a laboratory, but in our daily routine of life. That's why Paul says in Ephesians 5, '*Live* and find out what pleases the Lord.'

Our focus is going to be on Colossians 1, and the section that begins at the ninth verse. Look first of all at verse 10.

If you have the NIV, you will notice that there is a colon after the word 'way'. It introduces a series of clear statements concerning the life that pleases God. In Ephesians 5:10 he has said 'Live and find out what pleases God,' and as we search the Scriptures in order to come to that understanding, we find ourselves here in Colossians. This provides us with a succinct opportunity to capture that understanding in four phrases, which I would like to bring before you now.

What are the marks of a life that pleases God according to this little paragraph?

First of all,

Fruitful living pleases God

'Bearing fruit', verse 10b, 'in every good work'. Sometimes we hear people referred to as being 'good-for-nothing'. That's seldom if ever true, but we may sometimes say it of ourselves. We look at ourselves physically in the mirror, and in the mirror of God's Word spiritually, and we wonder what we are on about.

We are, this phrase reminds us, in Jesus Christ, redeemed, born into the family of faith. All our days and all our deeds are to be good for something, and good for someone. So we have the direct, divine responsibility to awake to a new day, and in this day to write across our diaries, 'Today, I will find out what pleases the Lord.' And fruitful living pleases him. Therefore, all of my day and all of my deeds, may I so live as to be good for someone, and to be good for something. We cannot separate faith from faithfulness.

Wasn't it Luther who said, 'It is faith alone that saves, but the faith that saves is not alone'? We're experts, us evangelical Christians, at quoting Ephesians 2:8–9, because we're so concerned to make it clear – as it must be

– that we cannot add one iota to our salvation, that all we bring to it is the sin from which we need to be forgiven.

But we often leave off the tenth verse; not simply in our memorising, but, I want to suggest to you, in our living. God has good works for us, He says, fore-ordained for us to do. And He redeemed us in order that He might make us fruitful.

Is it not true that when bereavement comes to a home or to a neighbourhood, sometimes those of us who know what we should do and could do are run over in the crush by our secular unbelieving neighbours, who are carrying the soup to the door, ironing the shirts, and driving the children to school. And we excuse ourselves with the offer of a book or a tract! Do you remember what James said about that? He said, 'What good is it?' (James 2:16). It is no good at all.

I've heard all these people talk about 'the social gospel'. I didn't know what the social gospel was, but now I do. It was the notion that somehow, we put aside biblical truth and we sacrifice the underpinnings of the gospel for a kind of do-gooder activity.

It's a dreadful heresy, compared to what the Scriptures teach. But there is another dreadful heresy, and that is to divorce our theological foundations from our social implications. We may sit in this tent, and take our notes, and wave our books, and sing our songs, but there is a world out there that needs to know Jesus Christ. There is fruit in your life that may be picked by those who would long to see that life.

And that may happen. They do not understand our talk about how we have been 'raised to the heavenly places with Christ'; they do understand when we give them a cup of cold water when they're thirsty, and a lift in the car when they're weary, and a word of encouragement when they're lonely.

Let me give you a little bit of homework under this first heading. Read John 15, where Jesus speaks about the nature of fruitfulness, and you will discover that there is a dependence that fruitfulness displays and a discipline that fruitfulness demands. Remember, Jesus said, 'Apart from me you can do absolutely nothing.' What pleases the Lord? First, fruitful living. Secondly,

Knowledgeable living pleases God

'Growing in the knowledge of God'. The context in which Paul was writing was one in which people were suggesting that there was a mysterious knowledge to be gained only by those who had entered into this new dimension of life. It was a kind of gnosticism. And Paul wants to say to them, 'Listen, if you want to be concerned about knowledge, be concerned about the knowledge of God!'

He wants to refute the superstitious theories of the unbelievers, and he wants to deal with the secretive heresies of the gnostics. He wants to say, 'Part of your birthright in Jesus Christ is that you know God, and part of the evidence that you know God is that you are wanting to know Him more and more.' Isn't that what a child does with his dad or with his mum?

One of the things my children ask me again and again, when I tuck them into their beds, is 'Tell me something funny that happened to you when you were little.' Why do they ask that? They want to get inside of who I am. That pleases me, I love it when they ask.

Have you got that kind of longing after God? Not longing after Bible notes, but God. You don't want to read my diaries, you want to read my heart, you want to read my eyes, you want to read my hands. What pleases the Lord? A knowledge of the living. A knowledge which is first of all personal.

In the sixties all the pop groups had fan clubs; maybe they still do. They had little booklets that they sent out, and kids in the school had them, and you could ask them, 'What about Manfred Man', or 'What about Paul McCartney', and they could rattle it off – 'Five foot eleven tall, blue eyes, he drives this kind of car, he lives in this kind of cottage, this is his favourite food, etc.' You would say, 'My, you must know him really well.' And they would say, 'Well no, actually, I have never met him in my life, I just learnt it all off by heart.'

It's a tragedy to have some kind of head knowledge of God, and never meet Him. What a dreadful thing to become increasingly like a tadpole for God, with a big swollen head full of facts, and a little tiny tail that moves us through the pond of our life. Do you know God personally tonight?

The knowledge is a personal knowledge, and it is a progressive knowledge. The old song went, 'To Jesus every day, I find my heart closer drawn.' Do you love Him better tonight, some of you who have stood up and said you have been to fifty Keswicks? I think you do, because many of you have spoken to me, and I have seen it in your eyes. Keep on! Because we are watching you, that you might grow in knowledge so that we might learn to emulate your example.

Thirdly,

Powerful living pleases the Lord

'Being strengthened with all power according to his glorious might'. Notice two things: how the power is *discovered*, and then notice how the power is *displayed*.

It is discovered in God's infusing our lives with all that He is. Filling the emptiness of all that I am. It's a tall order to please Him in every way (verse 10) is it not? It's a tall order if we are left on our own, to try to summon it up, but you see God never calls us to please Him without providing us with the energising power to fulfil our obligations.

People say that knowledge is power: it's a maxim that is true in the Christian life as well. Somebody once asked Dr Martin Lloyd-Jones what was the secret of his powerful preaching. He replied that it was careful preparation; that he knew God in his heart, and he knew the text in his mind, and he therefore spoke with authority.

Perspiration or determination will be inadequate for us in living the Christian life. Sufficient only is inspiration, the infusing of the power of God, being strengthened.

If you are reading the Greek New Testament, see if I'm right. It's *dunamoumenoi*, a present continuance. It means: present continuous infusing of God's power.

Do you ever see those human cannon balls? People who climb down a gun barrel, and somebody lights something at the far end, and everyone holds their breath like mad, and they come flying out – one *boom*, and then they're on their own. Is that what you think your Christian life is supposed to be like? One boom, and then you're on your own? Let me tell you something, it's supposed to be like this: *boom boom boom boom boom*, every day, *boom boom*. I'm not going to take off on a Boeing 707 if it's going to be one *boom* and then I'm on my own!

You are here tonight and you think you have got one good *boom*, and that's you? No wonder you've got a face like that! No wonder your Christian life's stale, no wonder you have no joy in witnessing – no wonder! It's the present continuous infusing of God's power according to His glorious might.

Oh, those resources of God put in the tiny little earthen pot of you and me! Why? So that people will be able to say, 'My oh my, isn't he or she somebody'? No, so that they might see that the transcendent power belongs to

God, and not to us. So that our children might see us grow in grace and in the knowledge of Christ. So that we might be honest enough to tell them, I can't live sixty seconds for God except that He infuses me in His power.

Where is it discovered? Well, it's discovered in God. How is it displayed? That is very interesting and very instructive. You will notice that Paul says that this power is ready to be displayed *in their lives*. Not in some dramatic display which will titillate the minds of men, but rather in endurance, great endurance and in great patience.

When God's power is at work in a life, there will be a quality that is heart-transforming and life-renewing. There will be a steady persistence, there will be a quiet confidence. I have no interest whatsoever in being controversial, but I want to say tonight that as I both read the New Testament, and as I apply God's word to my daily experience, I believe that the preoccupation with so-called signs and wonders is one of the great diversions of the end of the twentieth century, to take men and women's minds and eyes away from Christ, in whom is all His fullness given to us.

I have seen signs and wonders. I saw them in the long-stay hospitals in Edinburgh when I was there for two years. I have looked into the eyes of people in wheelchairs; I have not seen them get up and dance around the room, but I have seen God's power manifested through them *in that* they are unable to get up and dance around the room. There was a dimension about their lives, a spiritual geography such as I had never experienced.

Finally,

Thankful living pleases God

'Joyfully giving thanks to the Father'. For what? For the redemption we experience and for the relationships with the saints that we enjoy.

What a tragedy that so many of us have made it our aim in life to find out what pleases ourselves! We have a gospel that begins with man and his need, rather than God and His glory. Or are we making it our aim to find out what pleases other people, in a wrong way? Tonight I believe God would call us to take all our decisions, and all our desires, and all our choices, and have every one of them governed by this all pervading thought: 'I must find out what pleases the Lord, Whoever I am, wherever I go, whatever I do.'

You can go back from here to a bank, to a school, to a factory, to an office, to a kitchen sink, and you can please the Lord. You can be fruitful, knowledgeable, powerful, and thankful. Was it Wesley who said, 'Give me a hundred souls who hate nothing but sin, and love God with all their heart, and I'll shake the world for Jesus Christ.'?

Well, would you look at this tent?

Let us find out what pleases the Lord.

BELIEVING IS BETTER

by Dr Donald English

John 20:19–29

You will remember, I'm sure, that Jesus appeared to His disciples. The door was shut, and yet He came, and said, 'Peace be with you', and they were absolutely breathless with excitement.

For some reason, Thomas wasn't there. So verse 24 says: 'Thomas (called Didymus) . . . was not with the disciples when Jesus came.' So the other disciples told him, 'We have seen the Lord.' He said to them, 'Unless I see the nail marks in his hands and put my finger where the nails were, and put my hand into his side, I will not believe it.'

Thomas is one of the few people in the Bible who has found his way into modern English idiom. There aren't many times you hear people say, 'He's a proper Jeremiah.' I have never heard anybody referred to as a regular Obadiah, or a proper Habbakuk, or a typical Zerubbabel. There are a lot of reasons for not calling somebody a typical Zerubbabel! But we do know about doubting Thomas.

It's not really very fair. Thomas was a necessary disciple. You wouldn't like him on any of your church councils, deacons' meetings, or committees, because whenever anybody said a glass was half full, he always said it was half empty. Whenever anybody said how many people are here, he would tell you how many seats were empty. Whenever anyone ever said that the weather was good, he would tell you that there would soon be rain. He wasn't an easy person to have around.

But he was a very necessary one.

Right questions

He was the disciple who said what most of the others were thinking but didn't like to say.

Thomas asked the questions that needed to be asked
It is so in John 11, when the news comes about Lazarus being ill, and Jesus inexplicably – as far as the disciples are concerned – says: Well, we'll wait a few more days. Then he says, 'Let us go back to Judea.' They all catch their breath, but it's Thomas who says, 'Let us also go, that we may die with Him.' A splendid man to have around! Thomas, why do you have to say a thing like that? Because it might be true.

In John 14:4 it's even worse than that. It's one of those breath-taking moments when Jesus is trying to help them to understand that He is going away, He is going to a place where it is safe for them, and necessary for them, He's going to send another Comforter; and He says, 'You know the way to the place where I am going.' Everyone is caught up in this wonderful expression; but Thomas says, 'Lord, we don't know where You are going, so how can we know the way?'

You can almost hear Peter whispering, 'Shut up!' and John saying, 'My dear brother Thomas, that wasn't a very mellifluous expression.'

'Ah,' says Thomas. 'No, I don't understand, and I don't think it's right. He hasn't told us the way, and we don't know the way, so Lord, why pretend that we know the way, when we don't?' Do you know what verse would not be in the New Testament if Thomas had not said that? 'I am the way and the truth and the life. No one comes to the Father except through me.' How would we evangelists have managed without that verse? Thank God for Thomas who had the courage to challenge even the Master Himself with a robust, intelligent, enquiring, courageous mind.

In any case, Thomas wasn't entirely to blame in this story. Imagine the pressure on him when they all burst into the room. He is on his own, they have all had a marvellous experience, they all come bubbling, bouncing, shouting in, they can't believe it, and they are all talking together. 'Thomas, we've seen Him, the Master is risen! He spoke to us, the doors were shut, He came through them! He breathed on us, He said peace to us, Thomas, He's alive!'

Wouldn't you have wanted to say 'Wonderful! Marvellous! Yes, that's great!'? Thomas said, 'That's not good enough for me. I'll have to know for myself, it will have to be a personal experience of mine. That you have had it doesn't make it right for me.'

It's true; the fact that your parents were Christians doesn't make you a Christian. As Billy Graham says, if you are born in a garage that doesn't make you an automobile. Thomas had the sense to know that if this was going to be worth anything, it would have to be something about which he could say, 'I now know that this is true for myself.'

I wonder, are some of you really playing at church? You've been brought up to it, you've joined it, and when other people say all kinds of things are true, you nod in agreement. But when people start giving testimonies, you begin to wriggle on your seat. You dread the day when the pastor will say, 'Why don't you give yours?' You'd have to say, 'Same as hers . . . Same as his.' Because you haven't got one yourself.

I had two friends, both now gone to glory. They'd reached their forties, and he had held every post that it was possible to hold as a Methodist layman in the local Methodist church and Circuit. Late one Sunday night they rang their minister and said, 'We're not going to go to bed tonight until we know what it means to be converted.' They were fortunate in their minister. He said, 'Just stay where you are.'

He drove round to their house. There they were sitting one each side of the fireplace, Bible on their laps. He sat down and started with the sinfulness of human nature, the atoning death of Jesus Christ for their sins, His wonderful resurrection to assure them of new life, and the challenge to repent and believe in that hope. They knelt. And this Methodist minister, with all the practical experience of all the committees, at last found what it was about. I heard him give his testimony several times after that. He never managed to give it without breaking down. All the wasted years of playing at church!

My sister, my brother, whoever you are, however much you know, and however long you've been in whatever it is you've been in, if you cannot say, 'I know Him for myself,' that's a tragedy. Join Thomas who said, 'Even though you can sing these marvellous hymns and choruses, I'm not going to believe it until I know it for myself.'

Thomas knew what he was asking for

He was right in another way. He knew what he was asking for. He didn't say, 'What did He look like?' He didn't say, 'Did He have the same voice?' He didn't say, 'Did He break any bread? Did He tell a story?'

He said, 'I want to put my finger in the mark of the nails, I want to put my hand in his side.' You may be critical of Thomas, but I guess he could teach most of us a whole lot of things, because Thomas was saying, 'If it's real, this appearance, it will be crucified.' Do you see? 'If it's the real Jesus, it will be the Jesus who died, won't it? So, I don't want to see Him with His face, I don't want to hear another story, I just want to be sure that what you've seen is my Lord, crucified on the cross.'

I wonder whether part of the trouble for some of us is that we are brought up on Jesus as friend, Jesus as shepherd, Jesus as alive, Jesus as example. None of that, to be frank, is worth very much, if He isn't Jesus as Saviour. The problem that He came supremely to meet was our sinfulness, not our loneliness. His primary reason for coming wasn't to make it possible for us to say, 'Whoever else abandons me, I'll still have Jesus.' He came primarily to bear our sins on His own body on the tree, so that we being dead to sin might live unto righteousness.

My sister, my brother, have you got as far as Thomas, when he was asked those questions? Do you understand that He is only what God meant Him to be for you if He's your Saviour from sin? Let me ask you, what do you do when you know you've said or done or thought something that was wrong? If the answer is not, 'I ask God for forgiveness through Jesus', then maybe you'd better join Thomas at the questioning stage. 'Are there wounds in the hand? Is there a mark in the side?' says Thomas, because that would be the authenticating factor.

Have you ever taken Jesus as your Saviour?

Thomas wasn't playing games

When Thomas set forth his terms, when he announced what he wanted to happen, he wasn't just covering up an unwillingness to believe in Jesus. When Jesus offered him what he wanted, that was enough. He wasn't hiding behind questions, he really wanted to know the answer to the question.

Do some of us, I wonder, hide our sub-standard Christianity under a cover of playing at questions? You know the kind of questions I mean. Intellectual problems, moral problems, philosophical problems, problems with the Church. Of course I don't mean that those questions don't have any intellectual, philosophical or theological validity, or that they may not reflect very real searching. I simply mean that many of us hide behind convenient problems of that kind, instead of being open about it and saying, 'The real truth is, I don't want to be wholly given to God in Jesus Christ.'

If that were the case with Thomas, he would have said so. Are you as honest as Thomas? Am I? Or am I glad when I have got an intellectual problem or two, when I find that there are some moral issues that I can't quite understand? Am I grateful when somebody gives me another philosophical objection so that I don't have to give myself whole-heartedly? Thomas was ready to respond when he received the evidence.

Wrong choices

But Thomas wasn't altogether right. He had some things wrong. Firstly,

Thomas wasn't with the disciples when Jesus came
Where was he? I hope you notice in verse 24 that John calls Thomas 'one of the Twelve'. Do you see the significance of that? One of the Twelve was not with them when Jesus came. You wouldn't have expected it from one of the others, but John can't believe the absence of one of the Twelve. Where was he? Had Thomas the doubter discovered that the glass was half empty after all? Had he, with his down-to-earth attitude, realised that there was no point in continuing, it was all dust and ashes now? Was he the first to make the break, voting with his feet, as we say?

'Oh Thomas, if only you'd been there, you would have seen Him.'

If there is a book in heaven, I wonder whether sometimes it says, Donald English wasn't there. Do you remember the day you were too tired to say your prayers? The day you decided that Bible reading is not really as necessary as you thought? The time you decided that the fellowship could be given a miss on this occasion? The day you become so sophisticated that you don't need to go to worship every week?

There's a process by which you stop trying to make Godly sense of the world, and just allow it to start invading your house and life and work. When you look at the standards of other people and say, well, it's the only way I'll ever get on. Bit by bit, you are not there, when Jesus comes. All His grace is available, but you are somewhere else. Oh Thomas, the trouble you would have been saved if you only had been there! My sisters and my brothers, I wonder if you need to repent of inadequate presence where Jesus is when He is trying to bless you.

I wonder how many of you need to covenant with God tonight – never again to give up on prayer and Bible study, and fellowship, and making Godly sense of the world – because when He is there, you aren't?

That's how you start slipping away. The pastor comes to see you, and you say, 'I don't know pastor, I don't seem to have the conviction once I had, you know.' Of course you don't. If you're not there when He comes, how do you expect to know He's there?

Sometimes, it's more subtle. Sometimes we are there, we are at the meetings, we do read our Bibles, we do say our prayers, we do go to church, we do attend the fellowship, we even hold jobs in the church. But we know within ourselves that all that is no longer the primary commitment of our lives. We know that now somehow something else – our spouse, children, getting on, money, ambition, leisure – is on the throne.

We still go through the motions, but the life isn't there. It isn't invigorating any more. It doesn't excite us any more. We don't find ourselves wanting to stand up and say, 'Hallelujah, preacher, that's right!' – we just sit like ducks and make conversation afterwards. Of course we can't just slide away quickly to watch the TV, or whatever it is that's got our heart. But we're sitting there in the sermon, and whatever it is that we're thinking about, that's where we really are.

Oh sisters and brothers, be there when He comes. Otherwise you will certainly lose faith. Of course you will. But if you do, don't blame God.

Thomas was not there when Jesus came.

Thomas had no right to make that demand of Jesus
Thomas had something else wrong. He had no right to talk like that in the first place. How can you talk so to God who made the hills and the valleys?

The Psalmist talks about the hills and the valleys praising Him. Have you ever asked yourself how hills and valleys praise God without a mouth? The hills praise God by being hills. The moment hills become valleys, they'll stop praising God. The moment the rain starts falling upwards, the moment the sun starts wetting you, the moment the snow is warm, the moment babies start being born at an old age, then things will have gone wrong; but until then, the hills praise God by standing in their might, and the valleys by being deep, and the seas by flowing, and the grass by growing, and the flowers in their colours, and the animals by running, and the birds by flying, and the fish by swimming. Everything praises God.

Only human beings have the choice.

Thomas, dare you face the Lord of all of this and say, 'Unless . . .'? I've been to Buckingham Palace, twice –

and to garden parties. Mind you, there were 7,999 other people there! But supposing the invitation had come, and I'd written back and said, 'Your Majesty, thank you for the invitation. I won't come unless my wife can have a room in the Palace to change and we can stay for dinner. And it would be helpful if you could provide a bed for us for the night.' Have you ever heard anybody replying like that to a royal invitation? It would be the best way to get yourself into the tower!

People say that's ridiculous. But imagine turning to the Lord of all the glory that's round about us, all the ions, the planets, time itself; here's little Thomas saying, 'God, unless . . .' How dare you, Thomas!

We're talking about Jesus here, the One in whom, the Bible says, God was pleased that all His fullness should dwell (Col. 1:19). Can you picture that, Thomas? The writer to the Hebrews says, He is the very essence of God (Heb. 1:3, NIV 'exact representation', RSV 'very stamp of his nature', etc.). It's a word that means, the 'very heaviness' of God. It's in Jesus. 'He who has seen me, has seen the Father, Thomas, Philip, all of you . . .'

How can you say, 'Unless . . .'? He has gone to the cross for you. He has given royal blood for you. The Son of God has died in your place, Thomas, and you say, 'Unless'. And He's risen from the dead, He's broken the power of death. Death is defeated, Thomas! That's what these people are telling you. Do you say, unless? What are your 'unlesses,' what are your conditions? Before the God who made everything, there are no 'unlesses'. That's what Thomas found.

Jesus came. This suffering compassionate love, that we have kept coming across in this Convention, here it is again. 'A week later' – not the next day, because Jesus wanted it to be exactly as it had been for the others. One week later, the doors locked; and in He came again. 'Peace be with you!'

That's what He said before, Thomas. You are going to miss nothing from a week ago. How gracious God is! But then He says, 'Now, what was it you wanted, Thomas? Hands? Side?'

Now, I don't think that Thomas ever did put his finger into the hands. I think that, because although Thomas's conditions were 'unless I see . . . unless I touch', a little while later Jesus said, 'because you have seen'. He doesn't say 'because you have touched'.

I think Thomas realised that he was in the wrong league. He realised that his conditions were not at all necessary. So he simply said, 'My Lord, and my God.'

Lord and God

You've got it right at last, Thomas! 'My Lord and my God'. 'Lord', meaning: every part of me is now available to you. Can you say that to Jesus? 'Every part of me is now available to you.' That's what 'Lord' means. And it means something more that we often forget. 'Whatever you did, I will seek according to your will, to do.'

We forget that. We offer ourselves, as it were; our personal possessions, our inwardness, we offer to Him. But Jesus was the One who went to the poor and the lonely and the needy. He was the One who turned human values upside down. He was the One who reached out to ordinary needy people, and they found He understood them. That's what having Him as Lord means as well.

That's why any dichotomy between 'the simple gospel' and 'the social gospel' is a nonsense. Jesus is the heart of both. He reached to the poor, the needy, the outcasts, the tax collectors, all the people the religious people would have nothing to do with. Jesus went to them. To say 'Lord' is to commit yourself to that. I wonder whether you have ever done that?

And 'God' is not just a synonym for 'Lord'. It is something different. 'Lord' draws attention to the 'me' whom He has a right to possess; but 'God' draws attention to the 'He' who is everything. Therefore, to say 'Lord' is to say 'Everything I have and am is yours'; but to say 'My Lord and God', is to say 'Everything that I have and am is yours, in doing whatever, O God, you want to do in the world.'

That's much better, because it's being enlisted into the kingdom. It's being called to serve Him wherever it might be. David Pawson once said, 'The world is God's, and He wants it back.' And He has called on His people to get it back for Him.

So to say 'My Lord and my God' is not simply to say, 'From now on, everything I have and am is yours.' It's to say, 'Everything I have and am is yours, in the doing of your will, Oh God, in all the world.' That spreads out into every part of life. It's about getting involved in life, for the establishment of the Kingdom. Have you ever thought of it like that, or is your Christian faith still highly personal, highly individual, and – I have to say it – largely for your own benefit?

Thomas, you're living on a big, big screen. That's why Jesus says, 'Have you believed because you've seen, Thomas? Happy are those who have not seen, and yet believe.'

Whatever does that mean? It means, you see, that if you can believe without seeing, then you're no longer tied to seeing. You're no longer tied to time and place. You don't have to have a regular appearance of the physical Jesus so that you will go on believing. You just take off into the timeless wonder of a belief that doesn't need to see.

There are so many earth-bound Christians! They're constantly needing injections. They're what Bill Batt from the UCCF camp used to call, 'filleted Christians'. They've got no back-bone. They can't fly anywhere, they can't stand on their own, they've got to lean on a lot of other people, and other people move away.

But Jesus is saying, 'Thomas, what you have discovered now is priceless, because if you can believe without seeing, you are into the new world of eternity, Thomas. You'll fly and fly and fly, because everything is now open to you. The world is yours.' That's why Jesus said in Luke 14, 'If anyone comes to me and does not hate father and mother, his wife and children, his brothers and sisters – yes, even his own life – he cannot be my disciple. And anyone who does not carry his cross and follow me cannot be my disciple'(Luke 14:26–7).

Not 'cannot be a good disciple', not 'cannot be a special model' – no: 'cannot be *my* disciple'. Why? Because what is being spoken of is the attitude of 'Lord, everything I have is Yours' – and that's real freedom. Once you possess nothing, because it's all in His hands, you are free as the air.

Do you feel like that? Would you like to feel like that? Well, before you leave this tent, say to the Lord, 'Lord, I'm finished with all these excuses, I'm going to be there when You come. Lord, whatever I have and am, insofar as I am able, I give it all to You. Lord, I am committing the whole of myself to whatever Your purposes are in the world; and Lord, You don't need to keep on appearing to me, so that I may see You. I believe. And believing, I fly to glory.'

Believing is better.

THE SAVIOUR'S LOVE-GIFT

by Rev. Philip Hacking

John 14:15–17

It's a truism hardly worth saying on a Keswick Convention platform, but I say it nonetheless, that if we love somebody well, we give to them, within the limits of our ability and our Christian stewardship, as generously as we can. You give a lovely love-gift. You give some flowers or a massive box of chocolates, you treat them to a concert, give them a free ticket to a Sheffield Wednesday match! – all the most precious things that the world can afford. And you show how much you love. You generously give because you love.

As I read these last words of Jesus in John 14, I see the Saviour offering the greatest gift, out of a heart of love. That greatest gift was His Son. And the Son and the Father give the Spirit as their greatest gift: another Counsellor, the love-gift of Jesus.

For it's quite clear in John 14 that the disciples, understandably, were troubled. They were troubled because the future seemed so uncertain, and my guess is that we're like that. Indeed, sometimes we come to Keswick and the ministry of the Word begins to trouble us more than we were before, because the Word of God has brought its searchlight into our hearts. And we feel even more troubled, because we're beginning to be aware of things in our life that need sorting out. Tonight is Thursday, when in our sequence of teaching through the week we think of the working of the Spirit. I always hope that Thursday night brings the beginning of hope and joy and liberation, if it's not come already. Jesus knows that we're troubled.

The disciples were troubled because He was about to leave them. There were two horizons that bothered them: there was what I call the *last tomorrow* – that realisation that we have mortal bodies and there's a last tomorrow. And Jesus speaks about that. He's coming again, and when He comes again there is all the glory and hope of heaven we shall share with Him if we're in Christ.

That's wonderful; that's a comfort. But sometimes it's the *next tomorrow* which is the greater problem.

The disciples weren't really bothering too much about the distant horizon, but about the near one. I'm sure we're all alike in this. Don't we all have things on the horizon, and say to ourselves, 'When I've got over that, everything will be marvellous'? It's that hump on the horizon. Whatever form it takes, it's something that makes us fear about the future, and we believe that beyond it, everything will all be level and plain. It's never true, is it? There is always another peak after the one you're climbing.

Jesus wants to say, regarding those 'next tomorrows', that He is promising them another Counsellor. He could even say in 16:7, 'It is for your good that I go away.' And the one who makes all the difference in the next tomorrow is the Spirit.

Now let me just go a stage further. When we talk about love-gifts, we don't always realise that the greatest love-gift is not that which satisfies me selfishly, but that which enables me to be a better person. And the Holy Spirit is not given by Jesus so that we might just go out and feel good. The Holy Spirit is given so that we might go out and bear witness (15:26–27, in this same block of teaching); He will bear witness and you will bear witness.

The last words of Jesus (Acts 1:8) were: 'You will receive power when the Holy Spirit comes on you; and you will be my witnesses.' And many people, when they think of power, think in terms of feeling, in terms of a great sense of dynamic within them. But no – the dynamic is there so that we might go *out*.

Let's just stay with that, because I believe it to be tremendously important. The meaning of a Convention is not just what happens when we're here, but what happens when we've gone out of here.

Do you sometimes get a gift that you think includes a hint? Your wife buys you a pair of gardening boots for Christmas, or a new sophisticated alarm clock for your birthday, and you think 'Maybe she's telling me something!' The worst of that type of present – may I say it to the hundreds of you tonight who are members of congregations – is the lady or gentleman in the church who gives you a book at the back and says, 'Vicar, I think you ought to read this.' You get the hint. 'There's something in that book for your good'!

Did you have to write thank-you letters when you were a child? The most difficult thing was avoiding being hypocritical. You know, your aunt would buy you a pair of socks. It was called a Useful Gift; there was nothing worse than getting a Useful Gift. And you wrote that awful letter, which was true and yet not true: 'Thank you so much; they will come in useful.'

But the Holy Spirit isn't coming in to be useful, He's coming in to make us useful. And as I look at these verses with you at the close of this evening, at the climax of our teaching ministry as we prepare to gather around the Lord's table tomorrow, I want you to believe that when Jesus talks of the Spirit as His greatest love-gift to you and

to me, the first thing I can point out is the context of the
Spirit's coming.

The context of the Spirit's coming

In the Communion Service of the new Anglican *Alternative Service Book*, we make three acclamations: 'Christ
has died', 'Christ is risen', and 'Christ will come again.'
May I point out to you, all the teaching of Keswick is there
in those three great phrases.

Christ has died

On Tuesday night we thought of all the glory of the
sacrifice of Jesus, without which there could be no Spirit.[1]

John 7:39 tells us that the Spirit had not been given
'because Jesus was not yet glorified.' John 14:6, 'I am the
way, and the truth, and the life' – we were reminded last
night of Thomas's question that prompted that verse.[2]
Thank God for Thomas! There could be no giving of the
Spirit till Jesus had died to make it possible.

And what the Spirit does in all our lives is to make real
in our experience the truth of Calvary. There aren't two
experiences, a 'Calvary' one and a 'Pentecost' one. The
Spirit makes Calvary real to me.

Now that's tremendously important. It's at the foot of
the cross that I receive the Spirit. Do you remember, in
Ezekiel 37, that story of the dry bones? And do you
remember that bone came together, bone to bone? There
was a sort of respectable corpse, but no breath. Then the
Spirit came.

And I liken all that to the fact that your life and mine is
made new at the foot of the cross. He brings the broken
pieces together. And the Spirit applies that to you and to
me. For, you see, it's very possible to believe in the
doctrine of the atonement, and to believe that Christ died

for me, but only the Spirit can actually make the implications real.

Christ has risen

'Christ has risen.' That comes out in John 14:2 – 'I'm going back to prepare a place' – again in verse 28 – that 'I'm going away, you should rejoice.' He's risen, He's going back to the Father. That's His promise. And the Spirit is the first-fruit of the ascended Lord.

So now we can pray (cf. verses 13 and 14) because our Lord's at the right hand. We can pray in the name of Jesus, and, Romans 8 tells us, they tie together; the Spirit within us prays with groanings that cannot be uttered. He helps us to pray.

Because Christ has risen the Spirit brings within us the reality of the lordship. How can we live the lordship of Christ in our daily life? Only by the Spirit. And you should be eager to go out, because you have within you the Spirit that enables you to proclaim, by life as well as by word, 'Jesus is Lord'.

Do you find that phrase in 1 Corinthians 12:3 odd – 'No one can say "Jesus is Lord" except by the Holy Spirit'? Surely, there *are* thousands of people who say 'Jesus is Lord' and don't mean it?

No; what he really means is, 'Nobody can proclaim that truth with conviction and integrity without the Spirit of God.' If you want to live out that lordship you need that power of the Spirit – but you've got the love-gift.

Christ will come again

In the English version that I have in front of me, that lovely promise in verse 3 is made up, apart from one word, entirely of monosyllables. It's a lovely sentence. Beautiful simplicity. It couldn't be clearer. The message of Jesus is that we shall be with Him, if we're in Christ. He will come again – and the New Testament insists that the Spirit is the pledge.

I'm tempted to use the illustration of the engagement ring, but I've told it so often at Keswick that I daren't tell it any more! I think I may be allowed to say just this, however. The analogy of the engagement ring appears in 2 Corinthians 1:22. It is the 'earnest', the 'pledge'. The word *arrabōna* in the Greek is the modern Greek for 'an engagement ring'. The message comes out loud and clear: the engagement ring is a pledge of another ring to come; you're not just engaged, you're going to be married.

The engagement ring is a foretaste of the wedding ring. It's a marvellous truth. There's a 'not yet'. Paul writes 'For now we see through a glass, darkly; but then face to face' (1 Cor. 13:12, AV). 'Now' we live in our mortal bodies, 'then' there is no more pain, no more sorrow. And how do I know that I'm going to get to the 'then'? Because He's given me the engagement ring. And I know if He loves me enough to give me His Son on the cross and the Holy Spirit in my heart, He won't let me down.

I was talking to an elderly lady in her nineties the other day who was an atheist. I thought it was time to have a word with her about what might be happening soon in her life. And she said to me, 'Supposing you're wrong?'

'Oh,' I said, 'you've let yourself into trouble now; supposing *you're* wrong?'

But you see, how *do* I know I'm not wrong? How do I know that that day will dawn? Well, the Word says so and the Spirit in my heart bears witness it is so. I've got the engagement ring! Christ will come again!

That's the context of the Spirit's coming – Christ has died, Christ is risen, Christ will come again. And the Spirit always comes to bear witness to Jesus.

The confidence of the Spirit's coming

Now, secondly, may I point out to you the three words used of the Spirit? Our confidence is all to do with who the Spirit is. And there are three lovely names given to Him.

The Counsellor

First (verses 16 and 25), He's called the Counsellor, or the equivalent in whatever Bible version you have.

The word means 'the one who comes to represent God among us, to strengthen us, to enable us'. It's used in 1 John 2:1 of Jesus: He is our 'advocate' with the Father. He represents us in heaven, and the Spirit represents God in our hearts. And because of all that, we have strength to witness.

You heard the other day, that reminder[3] from Donald English that Moses complained, 'I can't speak', and God said, 'I'll be with your mouth' – so no more excuses, for we have the enabling. Jeremiah said, 'I'm too young' – 'But I will be with you, so I will take your immaturity,' God told him.

So there's the great promise. Think of that lovely moment on the Day of Pentecost when Peter, who'd failed the Lord so miserably in the Garden, was now able to preach the risen Lord because the Spirit had come as his Counsellor. Note that with Jesus yards away he made a hash of it; with the Spirit in his heart he had courage and power.

The Spirit of Truth

In verse 17 He's called the Spirit of Truth, and we're told in verse 26 that we will be taught everything, 'reminded of everything I've said to you' by the Spirit. Later, turn up one or two of the verses, from 16:12 onwards, where Jesus

promises the Spirit of Truth will lead us into all the truth –
for if we know the Spirit we know the Author.

I know all of us have been tremendously encouraged by
the morning Bible readings. I think it's important that you
should know that we who preach find such uplift from
being ministered to by others. You will remember we
were reminded this morning that only the Spirit of God
can interpret the truths of God.[4] So if I have not the Spirit
of God I have no understanding, but when the Spirit
comes He guides me, He interprets.

I sent my son a copy of my first book. His comment was,
'Yeah, okay – it was just you, Dad.' I took it as being a
compliment. Maybe it wasn't! But I think what he was
saying was that what came out in the book was the person
he knew.

I want you to believe that when you know the Spirit of
Truth in your heart, what comes out of the Scripture is the
truth of the person you know. You know the book, you
know the Author. How marvellous that is – the Spirit of
truth!

This is no platform for controversy, and God keep us
from it. But sometimes we do trivialise the whole idea of
wisdom and knowledge. It seems to me the Spirit of
wisdom and knowledge is basically the Spirit who enables
me to understand the mind of God, and to apply it to
those tremendously big things that Donald was reminding
us of this morning. And if several thousand of us saw the
possibility of being indwelt by the Spirit, of grappling with
the truths of our world, of standing up and speaking up –
that would do a lot more good than some of the things I
hear that are supposed to be wisdom and knowledge. I
believe it's deeper than ever we understand.

The Holy Spirit
The third, and obvious, name is the Holy Spirit (verse 26).
He is called that (verse 26) because He comes from God;

because He comes to make us holy; because He comes to work from within us (2 Cor. 3:18), so that we're being changed into the Lord's image from glory to glory by the Spirit.

And here's the liberation. If you've been challenged this week and you've opened yourself to Him – if you've been renewed in your mind and your heart – then you see what we're being promised is something very beautiful and very wonderful. That is, we have within us the Spirit. It's not that we're going to go away with a grim determination to do better (well, a little of that doesn't do any harm), but alongside that, within us, the *enabling to do it*. To make us holy.

May I again say, to become what we are, often *where* we are. Just before this year's Convention there was a lovely interview with Cliff Richard on television. He was so true, so genuine, so honest; thank God for him! I must say I wish that some of our church leaders had the same courage and clarity as dear Cliff Richard as he made his testimony. And he reminded us of the time when some were saying to him, 'Oh, now you're a Christian you can't just stay in the entertainment world! What about teaching?'

Now, I've no doubt Cliff Richard would have made an adequate teacher. He'd have reverted to being Harry Webb, which I gather was his original name, and we'd all have forgotten him by now. Don't get me wrong, teachers are very, very important people! But aren't you glad that in that tough world, he went back as a person indwelt by the Spirit to live it out there?

And I believe, from people I meet in these circumstances, that everybody, but everybody, acknowledges the genuineness of that man's life and commitment; that out of his life is seen the reality shining in a place where there's a lot of darkness.

Some of you may have heard about the conversion of
Glen Hoddle, the footballer. I've heard his testimony, and
I know that he is concerned that in that realm of sport
where he is well known, his new life within should shine.

I simply want to say, 'Thank God for changing that
man's life.' And I want to say this: that wherever we are –
and we're not in the limelight like those people – the Holy
Spirit can, in and through us, work out His holiness in the
world, which is where it's meant to be seen.

The consequences of the Spirit's coming

Now, finally, what are the consequences of the Spirit's
coming? What happens?

Three beautiful, simple things. And on this note we
end.

A new presence

That lovely promise (verses 16 and 17): 'He'll be with you
for ever . . . He lives with you and will be in you'. The
lovely picture on the day of Pentecost when the Spirit
came like a sheet of flame dividing upon each one of them;
one Spirit, but indwelling each one.

You cannot have the Spirit as your peculiar possession
and cut yourself off from the people of God. And though
the Spirit unites you with the people of God, you may not
say, 'Well, I belong to the Church, so I have the Spirit.'
No, no, no. He must indwell you personally, a new presence with you for ever in you.

Do you remember when Jesus talked to that rather
remarkable woman at the well? Another prostitute. He
talked to her in John 4. He had a marvellous conversation.
The woman begins to see He's talking about something a
little bit beyond her understanding, but she's feeling after
it; and He says, 'Look, I'm going to give you something so

that you won't have to keep coming to draw water. I'll give you water that will keep on springing up within you. It'll be in you welling up to eternal life.'

Listen, there are some Christians who are like that woman was, before she became a Christian. They rush around hither and thither for every new idea, every novel experience, every new message, every new personality. We're longing to find something out there that will solve our problems, and for a moment we're thrilled, and then we've got to go for something else – and then for something else – we're never satisfied.

There are some Christians who've forgotten, if they ever knew, that the source of their satisfaction is from within – the presence of God within like a spring of living water; a new presence, a new power (verse 12). 'Amen, Amen', says Jesus, 'I tell you the truth, if you believe in Me you'll do My works and greater works.'

A new power
Now, that means all sort of things. But what it does *not* mean is that we should forget that it's the same power that's linked with Calvary.

It does mean that we should expect God to be at work. It does mean that our lives should smack of the supernatural. It does mean that we should expect things to happen in our church that will demonstrate that God's alive.

A 'demonstration of the Spirit's power,' said 1 Corinthians 2:3 and 4 – and that was mostly in lives transformed and snatched from death. A new power, but the power is always the power of the cross; strength made perfect in weakness.

A new peace
There's been a theme running by God's grace through this Convention. It's been a reminder to us all that the message of love and compassion is the greatest power in the

world. And with all that goes a new peace – the promise there in verse 27, 'My peace'; and He promised in chapter 15 'My love' and 'My joy'.

Do you see it? Here is what you may have, here is this grace; not a package deal – I hate package deals! – but something more wonderful.

I've just got one minute more – I ask your patience. I would just ask you to ask yourself the question: Are you enjoying these realities in your experience?

Some time ago I heard an emergency message on the radio: Would Donald MacTavish (I tell this story often and get the name wrong each time), living in London and travelling the roads of London, would he please apply to the nearest police station?

Apparently there was a message there that would be to his advantage   But as I listened to that story, somewhere on the streets of London was a man living as a pauper when, in fact, he should be living as a prince.

That's not triumphalism, that's just you and me enjoying that which God gives us, so that we might live usefully. It's a love-gift. It's a useful gift.

Just as we close, I want you to think through. Do you know it? Is there, in any sense, some climax today in our week of teaching that will make tomorrow a new day, as you gather round His table?

Maybe you want to talk to one or two of us about it afterwards. We're around; we'd love to talk. But, most of all, simply say, 'Thank You for giving me Your Spirit,' make it your prayer, believe it and respond to it.

1. Of the two Tuesday night addresses on this theme, that by Rev. David Jackman is included in the present volume, p.175.
2. See the address by Dr Donald English in the present volume, p.195.

2. See the second of Dr Donald English's Bible Readings, p.32.
4. See the third of Dr Donald English's Bible Readings, p.50.

CHRISTIAN REALISM

by Rev. Gordon Bridger

Romans 7:14 – 8:4

Many of you will know that there is a progression through the week's teaching at Keswick. First the focus is on the glory of God, very often in the Sunday services, and then on the Monday it is on sin in the life of the believer. We move on to the cross of Christ on Tuesday, the lordship of Christ on Wednesday, and then the fullness and the gift of the Holy Spirit, and the resources of the Holy Spirit, on Thursday. And the week culminates in a lovely communion service on Friday.

Now, I don't want you to go away this Monday night with the impression that if God convicts you tonight, you've got to wait until tomorrow night before you know the healing, sanctifying, cleansing work of God through the death of Christ, through His blood, and through the Holy Spirit. But I do want you to see that there is some real value, as I and thousands of others have found, in taking time to let God focus attention upon our own lives, and upon sin (for that's our theme), in the life of the believer.

As we come together to listen to the Word of God, we look into the mirror of God's standards. We see, for example, the example of Christ. And we begin to see ourselves as we really are in the light of God's standards, and not in that of our own. And that in itself points us to the place of cleansing, to the cross of Jesus Christ, to that death which is for us, and that cleansing which is available for every believer; and I trust that that will be our experience tonight, as we look together into God's Word.

There's perhaps one other thing that I want to say in introduction. It's very easy, as we let God's Word speak to us about our own condition, to think 'That's marvellous, and I'm so glad So-and-So is here tonight' – instead of letting God say to us, 'That's just what *you* needed to hear.' It's the temptation of the preacher too: 'Now, how can I make the Word relevant to those to whom I'm speaking?' – whereas first we have to say, 'What is the Word saying to me?' For we all sit under that Word.

So as we sit and let God's Word speak to us, let's ask Him to speak to each one of us individually, and show us something about ourselves and something about our Saviour.

There are perhaps three general views about human nature.

There are those who take *a very optimistic view* – I mean people outside the Church – believing that human nature is essentially good, and that we only need better education, and a better environment, and our problems will be solved. But two world wars, and all the awful strife, terrorism, violence, and the rest of it that have gone on in what some think is the best-educated century of all time have made that kind of theory nonsense. I think there are very few people today who believe that man is essentially good. Some humanists and some Marxists do. But all around us we have evidence to the contrary. So it can't be an exclusively optimistic view, even though some would claim it is.

Others take *an exclusively pessimistic view*. They say that man is a useless passion. As someone said, it's meaningless that we live, and it's meaningless that we die. Man is on a hopeless disaster course, he's going to destroy himself. There are many people who think there is no hope or cure for man. Education, technology, science, improving his environment, have all failed. And an increasing number of people therefore live by the philosophy of 'Eat, drink and be merry: for tomorrow we die.'

But there's the third view, and it's *the biblical view*. It's not exclusively optimistic about man, and it's not exclusively pessimistic. It's what I would call *realistic*. And it's expressed in the words in Romans 7:24–5 that I want to take as my text tonight: 'What a wretched man I am! Who will rescue me from this body of death? Thanks be to God – through Jesus Christ our Lord!'

That's a realistic view of man isn't it? On the one hand, I'm able to say, 'Yes, there are times when I know and experience how wretched I am, wonder who or what can deliver me from my self-centredness, self-indulgence, indiscipline, rebellion.'

That's a fairly pessimistic view of my own human nature, but it's not exclusively pessimistic. The Apostle can also cry, in the same breath as it were, 'Thanks be to God – through Jesus Christ our Lord!'

There is a Deliverer. I may be pessimistic about myself, but I'm very optimistic about what God has done, and can do, to change my nature, and to make me into the kind of person that He wants me to be. That's a realistic view. I want to ask you tonight, are you a realistic Christian?

Let me develop that a little bit further from Romans 7. I believe Paul would have us focus on two truths in this chapter. First, that we should acknowledge that there is sin in the life of the believer, and, second, that towards the end we should see something of the fact that there is deliverance through the work of our Saviour. Those are the two truths that I believe Paul would have us focus on in those words in Romans 7.

Acknowledgement of sin in the life of the believer

Some will say 'Well, surely, Paul was not writing as a Christian. Would a Christian say, "Wretched man that I am! Who will deliver me from this body of death?" Those can't be the words of a regenerate Christian. They may be the words of a religious person who has no personal faith, but surely not a Christian!'

And it must be said that there are some commentators who would take that view – that Paul is not speaking here about his Christian experience, but his experience before he became a Christian.

But there are many other commentators who would argue that though that is true in Romans 1–13, from verse 14 onwards certain things change which suggest that Paul is indeed speaking as a Christian about his own Christian experience.

There is, for example – and it's often pointed out – a change of tense in verses 7–13. Before that he mostly speaks about what he was in the past. Now he begins to talk about the present. Verse 14: 'I am unspiritual, I do not understand what I do, for what I want to do . . .' – now – the present – '. . . I do not do, but what I hate I do.'

He knew something of that experience as a Christian. That's what many people believe is the significance of that change of tense.

There's a change of attitude too, to himself and to God's law, which doesn't seem typical of the unconverted, unregenerate person, the person who is not yet a Christian. Thus he can say about himself (verse 18), 'I know that nothing good lives in me.' Would you have said that before you became a Christian? Isn't that what a Christian has come to understand? That in myself, apart from God's grace, there is no good thing? That I'm still a sinner, even though I'm a forgiven one?

And Paul seems to be speaking about that in the present: 'I know that nothing good lives in me.' Or, verse 22: 'I delight in the law of God in my inmost self.' Or, 'I myself serve the law of God with my mind' or, in the NIV, 'I myself . . . am a slave to God's law.'

Here's a different attitude to the law. Would a non-Christian, an unconverted person, say 'I delight in the law of God'? Surely the very opposite is true. Indeed, Paul goes on in Romans 8 to say, in verse 7, that the unbeliever is hostile to God; he doesn't delight in God's law; he's often unwilling to admit he's a sinner. We know that ourselves from our own experience in the past.

Whereas the Christian, who knows what it is to have come to that point of acknowledging his or her sin, and has come to the cross – the Christian, by the grace of God, has begun to see how wretched he or she is in himself, and has also come to delight in God's law, and knows something, though often dimly, of a longing to do God's will and to keep His law.

So what I'm suggesting is that this is how Paul, an apostle, a mature Christian, sometimes felt; that sometimes he might have said this kind of thing. There were times when he lapsed, as we do, into trusting himself, in trying to live without constantly depending upon the grace and power of God, and in those moments he knew what it was to fail. He knew what it was again to be pulled down by his own nature. He knew what it was to say with honest Christian realism, 'Oh, wretched man that I am, who will deliver me?'

And I want to suggest that if my reading of the passage is true, it can be quite an encouragement for most of us, if we've experienced that kind of experience, or are experiencing it even now. It's an experience that the great apostle Paul also knew something about.

So, what's the reason for the Christian believer ever feeling like this – being aware of wretchedness, and crying out in this humble, contrite way?

Well, there are three things I want to draw quickly to your attention in Romans 7.

Indwelling sin

Earlier in Romans, as you know, Paul has demonstrated that all have sinned and come short of the glory of God; not only the wicked pagans, as it were, but also the moral pagans, and the very moral and religious Jews. Even those people who are justified in Jesus Christ, who have been accepted by God through faith in Jesus and are now united to Jesus by faith, even they are also sinners, though forgiven sinners; that their sinful nature was not eradicated when they became Christians.

And so in Romans 7:17 he says, 'If I do what I do not want . . . it is no longer I that do it, but sin which dwells within me,' or, as the NIV puts it, 'sin living in me'.

That's the first thing to acknowledge and recognise, that though I'm a Christian by the grace of God, born again by the Spirit of God, sin still dwells in me, my sinful nature has not been eradicated. Somebody once put it, 'We're all from the same mould, even if though some are mouldier than others.' A sinful nature, a tendency to sin, is still there in the heart and life of every person. The old nature has not been eradicated.

Inherent weakness

And, because of that, there is, secondly, not only indwelling sin, but indwelling sin leads to what I call 'inherent weakness', or 'weakness of the will'. It means what sometimes Paul calls, 'in the flesh'; depending upon ourselves, and not trusting and depending upon God and His Spirit. I know what he is talking about, for instance, in verse 18 – I have the desire to do what is good because of my new nature, but I find I cannot carry it out; I can *will* what is right, as one version puts it, but I cannot *do* it.

He's not saying exactly the same thing as would have been true before he became a Christian. Somerset Maugham wrote a book called *Of Human Bondage*, which tells the story of somebody (whom many believe to be Maugham himself) abandoning a very childish and rather impersonal belief in a deity, and becoming an atheist. He believed that thereby he could enjoy himself to the full, and discover liberty and freedom, untrammelled by God and religion and laws.

The novel describes some of the things he did to express that freedom. And it contains this description of his experience:

> He was astonished at the weakness of his will. It seemed to him he was swayed by every light emotion, as though he were a leaf in the wind. And when passion seized him, he was powerless, and had no self-control . . . He thought of what he was going to do, and when the time came to act, he was powerless in the grasp of instincts, emotions, he knew not what. His reason was someone looking on, observing the facts but powerless to interfere.

That, I believe, is a very perceptive description of the unbeliever, of the bondage of sin – *Of Human Bondage* – and of the way in which passions enslave.

But notice, the difference between that and what Paul is talking about here is that *he was powerless to intervene*. There was nothing he could do. And what Paul is saying is that in myself, because of my sinful nature, there's nothing I can do. But that's not the whole story! I am now in Christ.

So although we have to recognise that as Christians we sometimes slip back into trusting in ourselves, our experience, or (even in Christian work) our gifts, and so become once again powerless in ourselves, it's not the whole story. There *is* an inherent weakness – but only in ourselves.

But we still experience it, that's the point, that's the realism, isn't it?

We come to Keswick and we say, 'I realise as I come to hear God's Word that I need to take more time to read it. I want to do it.' And what happens? Time and time again we don't. Or we say, 'I want to give a proportion of my money, a tithe, to God's work.' And we don't. Or someone may be saying, 'I want to break off that relationship with somebody who's not a Christian. I know it's leading me away from Christ.' Or perhaps 'I want to speak out against injustice or dishonesty at work. I recognise that as a Christian I'm not to live only for myself; I'm called to be salt and light in society. I want to do it, Lord.'

'But the good that I want to do,' says Paul – as a Christian – 'I often don't do it.'

And let's be quite clear that 'sins of omission' have serious consequences just as 'sins of commission' do. The sin of neglect has caused enormous and widespread harm.

So Paul says – as a Christian – 'Because of indwelling sin, I have this inherent weakness in myself. Though I have begun my Christian life in the Spirit, turning to Christ, trusting in Christ, depending on Christ – though I began like that, like the Christians in Galatia, I've gone on, and I've forgotten to depend and trust. And so the things I want to do, I do not.'

Inward conflict
Indwelling sin leads to inherent weakness, and, thirdly, to inward conflict. And there's occasions when Paul makes

that plain, doesn't he? Young Christians often wonder why life sometimes becomes more difficult just after they become a Christian. Is that your experience? You thought everything was going to be fine. But instead you have all sorts of issues and temptations that you have never been bothered about before, issues you've got to decide about; and suddenly you find yourself with inner conflict. Well, so did the apostle Paul.

Verse 23: 'I see another law at war with the law of my mind which dwells in my members,' he says, speaking of the experience he had as a Christian. 'I know something', he says, 'of inward struggle.' I believe it continued throughout his life. He'd fought a good fight, he said at the end of his life – but it was a fight.

To the Christians at Galatia he said 'The Spirit lusts against the flesh and the flesh against the Spirit' (Gal. 5:17, AV). There's a battle, there's a conflict.

And then notice in verse 21: 'I find this law at work: When I want to do good, evil is right there with me.'

Can there ever be a time when you want to do good more than at Keswick, when you've got time to get away from the business of life and to be quiet, to listen to God's Word and to take it in, and to think about it, and reflect upon it? But here the apostle says, 'because of indwelling sin, when I want to do good, even then – that's when I most want to do good – evil is right there with me.'

I go back from the Convention at night to where I'm staying, and I find I say something, because I've been slightly hurt or offended, which I regret. I go back from Keswick home to a church, home or work situation, and I'm going back wanting to do right, but because of sin, I find that evil is right beside me.

Well, that's the kind of realism that the apostle speaks about in Romans 7, and I believe it is a description of sin in the life of the believer.

But, thank God, we don't have to leave it there.

There is a battle, there is a conflict, there is the evidence of the two natures and the inherent weakness in my own nature. But there's also the hint of the power and the difference that the new nature could make to me and the spirit within me.

Deliverance through the work of the Saviour

Now Paul goes on in chapter 8 to speak about the life in the Spirit. Verses 1–4 seem to be a summary. I want to look at those verses for a moment, because we've looked at the way in which we have to recognise sin in the life of the believer; now let's look at deliverance through the work of the Saviour: 'Thanks be to God through Jesus Christ our Lord!'

The deliverance comes in two ways: first,

Through what Christ has done for us on the cross
Paul has already talked about this a good deal in this letter, and he sums it up again here: 'There is therefore now no condemnation for those who are in Christ Jesus.'

God the Spirit is beginning to show us our weakness: the indwelling of sin, the inherent weakness in our own strength to do anything, and the absence in ourselves of anything that's good. We recognise that. It's the conflict that still continues as we go on in the life of the believer. What hope is there?

Well, first, there's no condemnation if you're in Jesus Christ. God has dealt with sin. The argument in Romans 7 deals quite a lot with the law. Paul has pointed out that the law, though good and from God, cannot actually save us. It condemns us. But, he says here, what the law was powerless to do (because it was weakened by the sinful nature), God did by sending His own Son in the likeness of sinful man to be a sin-offering, and so 'he condemned sin in sinful man'.

(I'm not too happy about that translation in the NIV, as a matter of fact; it seems very mild if it's saying that Jesus came to condemn sin in sinful man. After all, the law had already done that. I prefer the translation which says that God condemned sin in the flesh, and refers to the flesh of Jesus.)

There's no condemnation for those in Christ Jesus, because when we come to faith in Christ Jesus, when we're united to Jesus Christ, we're moved from that sphere which is under judgement; we are (remember Romans 6) dead to sin's judgement and its domination, and we're moved into a new sphere, in Christ, under the reign of grace, no longer under that of law.

And so in Christ, for all that the sinful nature, the inherent weakness in ourselves, is still there, there's no condemnation because Christ has borne it for us. God condemned sin and the consequences of my sin and yours in Christ on the cross. As Paul put it in 2 Corinthians, God made Him, Jesus, the sinless one, to be sin for us so that we might become the righteousness of God in Him, so that we might be accepted by God through faith in Christ (cf. 2 Cor. 5:21).

Oh, I know this is so familiar, but let this just thrill you again tonight. There's no condemnation! For the guilt and the shame and the judgement – all that we've recognised as sin within us deserves – has been borne by another; by Jesus. An old chorus that I love puts it well:

> There's a way back to God
> From the dark paths of sin,
> There's a way that is open and you may go in;
> At Calvary's cross is where you begin
> When you come as a sinner to Jesus.

. . . Because God condemned sin in Him for our sake in His great love.

Through what Christ is doing in us by His Spirit
What the law couldn't do, God has done something about, says Paul. He has sent His own Son as a man, living among us, living a perfect life, and giving His life as a sin-offering for us. And He condemns sin ('God condemns sin in the flesh', as I would read it).

Why? Verse 4: So that the righteous requirements of the law might be fully met in us. The law couldn't save us, and in ourselves we can't keep the law; but God sent His Son to die for us, and also to rise again, and to ascend into heaven, and by His Holy Spirit to enable us to live as He would have us live to fulfil God's law.

We look at the life of Jesus Christ and we remember that He kept God's law perfectly. And so we want to keep God's law perfectly; we long to be more like Jesus Christ in spite of the sin within us and all that pulls us down; we want to be like Jesus, we want to fulfil His laws, we want the just requirements of the law to be fully met in us and through our lives, despite the fact that we so often make resolutions and fail to keep them . . .

And we may well say, 'How can we be like that, like Jesus?'

I want to remind you that it would be a ridiculous notion – if you weren't one of God's sons or daughters. It *would* be ridiculous; but if you are a child of God, you have His nature, you have His Spirit, He's in you.

And that Holy Spirit, Paul says, enables you and me to subdue the old nature. He enables you and me to over-come this inherent weakness, so that what I want to do I can do in Christ. There's nothing I can do without Him, but in Christ I can do it.

The conflict that goes on within me, and will be within me until Christ comes again and I'm made like Him in glory, can be won. We can be more than conquerors over all the circumstances of life through Christ who loved us, if we're His children, because we are partakers and sharers in His nature.

So I want to close by asking: Are you a realistic Christian? Then you will acknowledge your sinfulness, and I will acknowledge mine: indwelling sin, inherent weakness, inward conflict. And if God has put His finger by His Spirit on any particular sins, then tonight, I'll want to confess them to Him and ask for His strength to forsake them. If we confess our sins, He is faithful and just to forgive. God wants us to deal with it tonight, to turn from sin tonight, to confess and acknowledge our sins tonight.

'LORD, BUT . . .'

Mr Dick Dowsett

Luke 9:49 – 10:2

Somebody told me they find this 'lordship night' a bit threatening; sometimes the enemy gives us that sort of picture, of a Lord who is an ogre who's really absolutely determined to muck our lives up. That's why some of you stayed away from this morning's meeting, isn't it – because you were terrified that God might be so rotten as to call you to be a missionary, and that really would wreck it!

I want to say to you, before we turn to the Word, that everything in the Bible tells us that the Lord loves His children, that's He's not there to wreck us, but to make us all that He wants us to be, and that He rules heaven and earth, and has that sort of commitment to crummy people like me, and perhaps more-or-less crummy people like you as well. So I want you to come for a gentle walk with me with Jesus, through part of Luke's Gospel, and see Jesus as Lord, and see the way that He wants to shape us up, together.

Please turn with me to Luke 9:49 – 10:2, and let's stroll along as if we were part of the disciples, on a walk to sort us out a bit, as was His habit with the disciples, who came to Him as they were, and were accepted as they were – but not to stay as they were; to be remoulded by Jesus.

As He walks with them, He begins to challenge them and us. And first of all,

Jesus challenges our ideas about what sort of people have commitment

They bump into someone who's casting out demons; but he's not one of their group, and that really puts John's nose out of joint, doesn't it?

'He *seems* to be being used – but he's not one of our group,' he said. 'So we tried to stop him, Master.' Poor old John! For him, commitment meant belonging to the right group, and it also seemed to mean fighting against other groups.

It's funny the way that people try to assess who's really committed to the Lord, isn't it? You notice this when you're a travelling speaker, because people check you out, and they want to categorise you to see if you quite fit their group, and whether you'll be all right. We categorise people as properly surrendered if they belong to the sort of group that we think is important.

Jesus won't kow-tow to that sort of categorisation, because Jesus looked at the man and He didn't ask what group he was in. He asked, 'Is this a man through whom I can get glory?' And it was.

We see a very beautiful insight here into the lordship of Jesus. It wasn't just that Jesus could do things Himself as He walked around at that time, but *He could do things through people who were available for Him*. Here, you see, people were being delivered from the power of the enemy by a bloke who was acting in the name of Jesus. Jesus had got a bloke he could use! No, he wasn't a regular, in the ordinary meaning of the rest of the disciples, but he was a man through whom people were delivered, through whom Jesus was glorified.

So the question Jesus is asking is, 'Are you a person through whom I can do things? Are you a person available for Me so that lost people can get right?' The Lord Jesus, because He is Lord, is able to work through people like that.

Some of us can be so busy fighting our inter-group battles and feeling that that's doing the Lord's work; but we're not really available for the love and the kingdom power of Jesus to flow out from us to a Satan-bound world. But that's what lordship is about.

Jesus challenges our ideas of how the Messiah ought to be

But then as we go on a little bit further with the disciples, they wander into a Samaritan village. And as they are there with Jesus, they see another problem about lordship; not a disciples' problem this time, but a Samaritan problem. It was the problem that when Jesus arrives, He challenges our ideas of the way that the Messiah ought to be.

If only Jesus had fitted with the Samaritan's ideas, if only He hadn't wanted to go off to Jerusalem of all places! Well, Jerusalem wasn't really quite the sort of place that turned the Samaritans on, was it? Jesus didn't fit with their prejudices, He didn't fit with the way that they would like to do things.

I wrote a book once on hell and judgement, entitled *God, That's Not Fair*. And sometimes people have written to me, saying 'My Jesus would never send anyone to hell.' *My* Jesus?

The trouble is that as you wrestle with the New Testament, you find that the Jesus who is there, who is real, doesn't fit with that sort of idea, and we can't have a Jesus who's tailor-made to our plans and prejudices. There's only one Jesus there, and He asks us to fit in with Him in

His teaching because He does actually know how things tick, and He does know what the facts are.

And here He is, on the move to Jerusalem.

Jesus challenges our longings for fire

I like what happens there, don't you? Here they are, these blokes, they go into the village with Jesus and they really think it's going to be quite a performance. Everybody's going to come flocking and say, 'Hey, isn't He the greatest,' because He is.

But they're not excited about Jesus, and they are probably pretty rude about it. And here's James and John, the Sons of Thunder, and they turn round at Jesus and say, 'Lord, do you want us to call fire down from heaven and destroy them?'

Maybe they'd been having their quiet time in 2 Kings 1, do you think? Because there you've got Elijah, in a bit of a hot water with the King of Samaria. The King of Samaria, you remember, sends two troops of soldiers – about fifty men with their officers – and the Lord vindicates Elijah and keeps him safe by sending fire from heaven. The soldiers are destroyed, they've had it.

And now the disciples are facing a Samaritan village that doesn't really want to be responsive to the Lord. So what do they say? They say, 'Do it again, Lord! Send the fire, Lord! Vindicate us, Lord!'

But actually, what they were saying was quite literally, 'To hell with the unresponsive.' And Jesus fair gave them a row. Here we see the Lord, the Lord of glory, who holds the fire in His hands, and what does He say? He rebukes them. Yes, it would have made that cosy group of believers more comfortable, it would have made them feel that they were sorted out, and that they were number one. And it would have done nothing for the lost.

Our glorious Lord who will judge all, He is slow to throw the fire. And He looks for a people who will walk with Him in compassion for the lost and for the unresponsive.

I suspect that there are some here tonight who find that difficult. Perhaps here tonight there are some whom we have sent out to other parts of the world, and you always assume that missionaries love the people that they go to, don't you? But sometimes it's very hard. Perhaps your house has been ransacked, perhaps they keep asking the sort of questions that you don't ask in England, that it's not right to ask in England. Perhaps they're not responsive, and it hurts. And it's hard to love, and it's easy to say, 'Oh, *blow* 'em.' Are you going to walk back there with Jesus?

I think of a Filipino missionary friend of mine who worked in Turkey. I don't know how many times he was in and out of prison, I don't know how often he was hounded by the police, I don't know what sort of traumas he didn't go through. And he's back home in the Philippines at the moment, and asking for prayer because he is so urgently longing to reach Turks for Jesus. You go on loving.

I met a man who cried with me in Thailand. He'd been working among the Muslims there. The Muslims aren't flocking to come to Jesus in South Thailand. There are about a hundred of them who are Christians among – what? – three million? And as he had worked among them they had put it around that he was putting curses on them. Their propaganda was so effective that eventually even the Christian believers and some of the Christian workers began to believe that it might be so. Can you imagine the awesome isolation of that? What they were doing to him because he'd gone to prepare the way for Jesus!

And how easy it is to want to wash our hands of unresponsive people, and the loving Lord, the Boss of the operation, says, 'Come on, that's not my way. I'm slow to anger, I'm slow to fling down the fire, because I'm not willing that any should perish.'

He challenged their longing for fire.

Jesus is concerned that commitment should be earthed in realism

And then we come on a little bit further and we're just outside the tent with Jesus, this morning, as it were, aren't we? Because you see, as they were walking along the road a man came bundling out – he must have come out of the Keswick tent, don't you think, on a Wednesday morning![1] And he says, 'I will follow you wherever you go.'

But after all, to say 'I'll follow you wherever you go,' isn't exactly graduate-level Christianity, is it? Is there anybody here who would *not* be prepared to say, 'I'll follow you wherever you go'? It's normal Christian commitment, isn't it? If you say, 'I'll follow you *here* and I'll follow you *here*, but if you're going *there*, I'm not coming,' you're a right wally of a Christian, aren't you? You are! Because *He'll* go that way, and you'll find an awesome far-offness in your relationship.

So here is a bloke who comes to the Lord Jesus, and says, 'I'll follow you wherever you go,' and Jesus is glad; but he is concerned that that commitment should be earthed in realism. And so do you see what Jesus says? He says, 'Yes, foxes have holes and the birds of the air have nests but the Son of man has nowhere to lay His head.'

What's Jesus saying? He is saying this, 'I've got nothing to offer you except Myself, I have got no guarantees except Me.'

Does that frighten you? You see, it does frighten us, because our concept of security and Jesus' concept of security aren't quite the same. We think we're secure if we've got the right kind of insurance policies, if we're more-or-less paid up on the house, and if we've got a secure job. Jesus' concept is different.

And again and again through the Scripture, when folk rather casually say: 'Oh yes, I'm committed', the Scripture says: 'Hey, wait a minute, do you know what it means?'

Poor old Isaiah at his missionary meeting, when God said to him, 'Who do you think I ought to send, lad?'! Isaiah said, 'Please may I go?' and God said, 'Yes. Let me give you the job description. Talking to this lot I'm sending you to is going to be like talking to a brick wall. They'll hear and they'll hear, but they'll not get it.' And as soon as he gets his job description poor old Isaiah said, 'How long, O Lord? Please can it be short term?'

And the Lord turns round and said, 'I want this job done until there aren't any people left in the houses.'

That's straight, isn't it? And the only hope that He gives him, the only thing to hang on to, He says, is that there's a stump and there's a holy seed, there's a Jesus who's going to win.

I used to say to people 'You go to the mission field and you'll prove all the Lord's provision,' and I still want to say that, because I've proved it so much. But, you might get killed. You might find the place ransacked. You might get very sick, you might get beaten up, you might get trapped into sin that you never thought you would. You might get forgotten. But you've got Jesus.

Now, when I say that to you, I hope that I'm speaking in the pattern that's given in the Bible. You've got Jesus and He's not going to spoil, but He knows the reality of this world, He knows the muckiness of it, He knows the hurting-ness of it. And the Lord of glory says, 'Yes, I'm coming down into the muck with you and I will really hold your hand. And the only guarantee I'm going to give you is my hand in yours, and I will not let go – not ever.'

Plenty others may muck it, but not Him. And He's the guarantee.

Jesus challenges our family life

Another bloke comes up and Jesus says to him, 'Follow Me.' And he says, 'Well, I'll do it when I've buried my dad.' There's no evidence that dad was already dead. 'Yes, well, this religious enthusiasm sort of thing, my dad's not really into that, and he might not really go along with it.' But Jesus has said, 'Follow Me.' In other words, Jesus as Lord challenges our family life.

I'm conscious that many of us need to be sure that we have biblical priorities about family life. I've been very deeply convicted, for example, that at the end of Ephesians it tells fathers to bring up their children in training and instruction of the Lord. It doesn't say it's a woman's job. There are too many Christian dads who hardly have time to talk for thirty seconds to their kids. I'm conscious of the fact that the Scripture says that if we don't provide for our elderly relatives we're worse than the pagans, and many of us ask the State to do it instead. So there are things that we, the British, need to sort out in that area.

But for some of us, our nice little family is the focus of our selfishness and our rebellion against the plans of God. How often I've had Christians say to missionary friends of mine, 'How dare you involve your parents in such sacrifice! How dare you involve your children in that!'

And I'm reminded that when Jesus in Mark 1:19 found James and John the sons of Zebedee, He told them, 'Follow Me, leave your nets.' Can you imagine poor old Zebedee? I mean, those boys were his pension plan, weren't they? Jesus knew all about Zebedee, and he said to the lads, 'Come on.' He said, 'Follow Me – not tomorrow, not Wednesday, when he's dead and buried, but follow Me today.' The Lord knows about the needs of our mums and dads.

I rejoiced recently in friends of mine whose parents were very sore when they went to the mission field, but who have recently come to Jesus. What about our children? Wicked to ask them to sacrifice? Do you think Isaac should have been carted off by the Social Worker after Mount Moriah? What a dad to do that! Ah, but the Scripture tells us, 'Your son, your only son, whom you love . . . says God'.

I remember when we come back from the Philippines and we were asked to move to Scotland, which nearly gave us a blue fit. It's more foreign to us than the Philippines for us, you see – we didn't know anybody there. And my elder son, who was then five, prayed one night as we as a family wrestled through this extraordinary call. 'Dear Lord Jesus, if you want us to go to Scotland please make it that we go and don't argue about it.'

That's Jesus as Lord. But that's not Jesus being beastly and rotten and sending us where we didn't know anybody; that is Jesus helping us as a family to prove the Lord in guidance, because when we got there that boy could write a letter, 'Dear Lord Jesus, you know that we need friends, and you've brought us here, so will you give us some?'

The kids can prove the Lord with the parents. But, you see, diluted discipleship is not good for our families, and if you say, 'I'll start living for Jesus when I'm free from family duties,' that's not what Jesus says here. He says, 'Come on, there is a priority which you must have, and it's proclaiming the kingdom.' And He draws our attention to the fact that there are so many things that we believers are busy doing that unbelievers can do perfectly well. But no unbeliever can preach the gospel.

Why is it that half of the world, as we thought this morning, has no opportunity to hear the gospel? The

242   Dick Dowsett

answer is clear, isn't it? Either it's perhaps because we haven't the priority of Jesus – to proclaim the kingdom – and have reduced missionary work to feeding pot-belly kids (which is important, but it's not the whole story); or it's because we're all busy sitting around our televisions enjoying family life.

Jesus doesn't ask you to let go of anything worth keeping

There's a last bloke here. He says, 'I'll follow you, Lord, but first let me go back and say goodbye to my family.' Now Jesus wasn't against valedictory services here. But he says to him, 'Stop looking over your shoulder at what you're missing, lad.' And that's a very important thing to understand.

The apostle Paul says that there are lots of very important things he's had to give up to follow Jesus; he says, 'I call them dung.' In the NIV they polite-ify it and they say, 'I call them rubbish.'

I want you to understand that it is very easy for us in our Christian lives to focus on what we once had that was good, which we've now got to let go of. You hang on to it – you'll be spiritually sick. Are you looking back at the things that you're missing now, because you're really trying to walk with Jesus? Are you resenting His lordship? 'Call it dung,' says Paul – or you'll be wrecked with bitterness.

There's one last thing that I want you to see. *Sacrifice is not sacrifice, when you let go of something that the Lord says to let go of, in order to move on in your service of Him* – yes, even if it's your beautiful little house. If you hang on to it it's like hanging on to dung. And you will be the loser. The Lord loves. He doesn't ask you to let go of what's good for you any more – even if it was good for you once.

Lastly, will you notice that the Lord sends out seventy-two people. You say, 'My isn't that wonderful! We didn't have seventy-two come forward at the Christian Service meeting this morning, but it wasn't bad.' But imagine — seventy-two new workers sent out in pairs, just for a weeny bit of Israel. That's not bad, is it, seventy-two workers! Wouldn't you say that's pretty good?

We find it so these days: people are saying to me, 'Well, isn't it wonderful, the Korean church is sending out workers,' and I was training people to go out from the Philippines as missionaries as well. There are more and more missionaries, because there are tons more people, and they're multiplying like mad in this world: there are more and more unevangelised.

But as seventy-two people are sent out, the Lord Jesus says to them, 'The labourers are few.'

The sweaty, gutsy torn-apart workers are *few*. And the Lord says one thing, and it challenges our way of getting things moving — it really brings into focus our concept of lordship: He says, 'Pray the Lord of the harvest to fling out the labourers.'

When my wife Rose was first called to the Philippines she said to the Lord, 'Who else?' and as she prayed, she drew up a list of thirteen other friends and she began to pray. A few years ago we had a phone call from one of them, and she said, 'I want you to know, I'm just leaving next week for Bhutan.' Rose put the phone down; she said, 'Praise the Lord, that's number thirteen gone — they've all gone now.'

The Lord says, 'Pray 'em out.' That one died just before Christmas. *Pray out some more*. Maybe you couldn't come forward this morning, because you can't go, but who's going to pray them out?

Will you ask the Lord what are the things that you've got to sort out, so that you can really walk with Jesus?

Don't say, 'Lord, but . . .' He's a loving, caring Boss, and He'll do it best.

1. This address was given on the Wednesday evening of Holiday Bible Week. On that morning the World View (Christian Service) meeting had been held, and the customary invitation offered to those who wished to make a public commitment to Christian service.

THE SPIRIT FOR OTHERS

by Rev. Robert Key

Acts 1: 1–8

We're going to look at Acts 1 together.

I want to preach a very basic sermon of four great truths which come to us from these first eight verses of Acts 1, about the person and work of the Holy Spirit.

It's like walking through a minefield, and so if occasionally an explosion goes off with your own theology, don't worry about it!

First of all, then, Acts 1:2

A personal Professor (1:2)

The Holy Spirit is a personal Professor. I use that word in its American context, to mean 'teacher' or 'tutor'.

Look at what we find the Holy Spirit doing as soon as He's introduced to us in the Acts of the Apostles. Read with me again: Jesus had been 'giving instructions through the Holy Spirit to the apostles he had chosen.' You say, 'Why did Jesus need the Holy Spirit when He preached? – I understand how a preacher does, because he preaches his heart out, and the Holy Spirit takes the preacher's word and applies it to the hearts and minds of those who listen.'

But Jesus was a preacher: He came preaching the kingdom of God; He preached and taught, and when He preached and taught, the Holy Spirit, the Trinity working together, took His words and wrote them in the hearts and minds of those who listened. So when we find Jesus taking the Holy Spirit and using Him as a teaching partner in His ministry, then we find Jesus being true to His own words.

John's Gospel (do you remember?): 'The Holy Spirit will take what is mine, and declare it to you.'

Jesus relied in His preaching and teaching ministry on the work of God the Holy Spirit.

You see, the preacher preaches his sermon, and then sits down, but the Holy Spirit doesn't let you off the hook. I can't sit with you all this coming week, and when something comes up in your life, dig you in the ribs and say, 'That's what I was meaning on Thursday night.' But the Holy Spirit can.

You were listening to the Bible Reading this morning. And you'll get back home to your churches, and maybe you'll have a lovely gossip session (oh, I forgot – in evangelical circles we call it 'sharing for prayer', don't we? 'I must just tell you this about So-and-So, so we can pray about it.' And all we are doing is gossiping with a holy face.)

And the Holy Spirit will dig you in the ribs, and says, 'That's what Mr Briscoe meant last week. So you can't do that now, can you?'

The Holy Spirit is our personal Professor, our personal Tutor, alongside us, underlining the teaching of God's Word in our lives.

I wonder if you have a recurring nightmare? I only have one, and it is that I fail an exam; for some reason, it's usually History A-level. Don't ask me why, but about once or twice a year, I fail History A-level.

Now, what I needed in the exam was somebody whispering in my ear, 'Spanish Armada, 1588; Glorious htht:.

Revolution, 1688', and all the rest of the dates I could never remember.

Well, the Holy Spirit comes in the Acts of the Apostles as a teacher, as a guide; because the word translated 'instructions' in verse 2 doesn't just mean theoretical teaching. It means practical instruction, marching orders – it's the word a commander might use as he gathers his troops together, and says, 'Right, lads, now we're going over the top: these are the commands that have been passed down from HQ, this is what we're going to do. And I'm going to be with you, leading you; I'm going to be there alongside you; I'll tell you when to point your guns; I'll tell you what to aim at, when to go, when to stop, when to retreat, when to attack.'

And that's the work of God the Holy Spirit as a personal Professor. His ministry to us is one that enlightens our minds, warms our hearts, and challenges our lives.

If you want an illustration of that, take that lovely story of the road to Emmaus in Luke 24. What do we find when Jesus has left those two disciples? They say, 'Didn't our hearts burn within us as he opened the Scriptures to our minds?' – and then they run back those miles to Jerusalem to share the resurrection with the disciples.

Their hearts were touched, their minds were enlightened, and their wills were changed. When God the Holy Spirit begins to be your personal Professor, then that's what He'll do for you. He'll teach you scriptural truth, and He'll nag away at you until you live like it.

A promised Present

Secondly, will you note that He is a promised Present. Look with me: 'Do not leave Jerusalem, but wait for the gift my Father promised, which you have heard me speak about' (1:4). 'Wait for the gift my Father promised . . .' –

it's interesting to note that Jesus just slipped this in over lunch – did you see that in verse 4? 'On one occasion, while He was eating with them.' You can just imagine the scene, can't you?

Now, this Present had been a long time coming.

Peter is going to quote in the very next chapter from Joel 2, where in the Old Testament God promises that one day He will pour out His Spirit. In the New Testament, in the ministry of Jesus, He promises in Luke 11: 'You . . . know how to give good gifts to your children. How much more will your Father in heaven give the Holy Spirit to those who ask him!'

And, in case we feel this is just something for the apostles, see how the apostles applied the promise of the Holy Spirit. Turn over to the end of Peter's Pentecost sermon (Acts 2:38–39); He's giving his altar call here: 'Repent and be baptised, every one of you, in the name of Jesus Christ so that your sins may be forgiven ['You are going to get saved'] . . . And you will receive the gift of the Holy Spirit. The promise is for you and your children and for all who are far off – for all whom the Lord our God will call.'

So the apostles took Jesus at His word, and said, 'Not only is the promise of the Father for us,' – but it's for all those who, in the words of John's Gospel, believe through their message. And when you believe, then God gives you, as part of the 'package deal' of salvation, the gift, the promised Present, of His Holy Spirit.

What sort of presents do you like for your birthday or for Christmas? When ask my wife, 'Darling, what do you want for Christmas?', she always tells me exactly the same thing: 'I want a surprise.' And so there am I on Christmas Eve, traipsing round the shops of Oxford trying to think of something she wouldn't think of.

But occasionally I get it right. One year I went to Laura Ashley and got her a dress. That was most unusual, because I can't even choose clothes for myself, let alone clothes for anybody else! But I got her a dress, and on Christmas morning not only was it the right size, but it was the right colour. And she said, 'It's just what I needed.'

God the Holy Spirit is just like that for each and every Christian believer.

It is God, who is sovereign, who gives you the Holy Spirit, and He gives you His gifts as He purposes, says St Paul: 'To each is given the manifestation of the Spirit for the common good . . . and he apportions to each one individually as he wills' (1 Cor. 7, 11).

Our part is to say, 'Lord, I want Your Holy Spirit in all His fullness, each and every day of my life.' And it's God's part – and today He's going to teach you this truth – to give you that gift, produce that bit of spiritual fruit. It's His work to give His surprise Present to His believing children.

Not only is it a surprise Present, but it is something which we have to unwrap. My mother tells the story of when she was a little girl. They weren't very well off. Each year her brothers and sisters – she was the youngest – clubbed together to buy her an Easter egg, preferably wrapped in beautiful purple paper, with a lovely purple bow around the middle.

She was amazed, year after year. It looked lovely, it was her favourite colour, it was exactly what she wanted, but she could never bring herself to open it and spoil the wrapper! So it sat on the shelf till the following Easter, when she had to throw it away because it was no longer any use.

God gives us His Present, but it's so easy for the Christian believer to want to keep the Holy Spirit 'under wraps', to want to 'tame Him down'. Do you remember that lovely bit in C.S. Lewis where the children ask, 'Is Aslan tame?' And the reply is, 'Tame? No, he's terrifying!' The Holy Spirit is like that, isn't He?

It's a lovely Present. We have to 'unwrap' Him. And you can get more than you bargain for.

Now, are you trying to keep God the Holy Spirit 'under wraps' in your life? Are you trying to say to God the Holy Spirit's power and holiness, 'You can't have that section of my life; I don't want you in there'? 'Unwrap' Him. Unlock that area of your life tonight, and allow His power, His presence, to transform you, and make you all that He wants you to be.

A permanent Possessor

Thirdly, He is your permanent Possessor. And I do mean Possessor, not possession. So often one hears said, 'The Holy Spirit is the permanent possession of the Christian believer.' No, He is not! You do not have God in your pocket, do you? He has you, not the other way round.

As long as you think you have Him, you'll think you're in control – you've got the rights, you're in the driving seat. But He's the one driving.

Look at the words used in Acts 1:4. 'John baptised with water, but before many days you shall be baptised with the Holy Spirit.'

Each school fete has its own traditions, and at my son's school fete they have a lovely tradition, which I haven't seen in other places. As well as all the usual stalls and bouncy castles for the young children, there are the medi-aeval stocks. Into the stocks they place not recalcitrant children who are late handing in their geography home-work, but teachers; and for 10p children can have five sponges soaked in cold water to throw at the teachers!

Half-way through the afternoon a few weeks ago at his school fete, the teacher who was in charge of the stocks had a bright idea. The 10p for five sponges got the staff fairly wet, but not completely, and so he said that for 20p the children could have not five wet sponges, but a whole bucket of water! They queued up twice round the running track!

Imagine yourself as a self-respecting classics master sitting in the stocks, and the person to whom you have just given three marks out of ten spends their last 20p, not on a can of coke, or an ice-cream cornet, but a large bucket of cold water. He or she advances, savouring the moment, and suddenly the bucket is inverted, and every tiny fibre of your being is soaked. It's gone down your collar, it's in your shoes, it's in your trousers, in your shirt – everywhere!

That's the meaning of the Greek word *baptizō*: 'soak to the skin'; completely drenched; no part left untouched.

Let's go with St Paul into the fifth chapter of Ephesians. There we find him telling the believers literally to be 'being filled' with the Holy Spirit, day by day. Not a once-and-for-all-at-conversion deluging, that perhaps *baptizō* gives us, but a daily filling of God's Spirit. The images of the Holy Spirit in the New Testament – and let's not make the mistake of holding a doctrinal battle over visual aids, which is what those words are – is that every area of the life of the Christian believer is to be drenched, deluged, soaked to the skin, in the power of the Holy Spirit which produces the character of Jesus Christ.

Every single area of your life and mine: nothing untouched; no dry socks; everything soaked.

Let's apply that a little bit, shall we?

In Ephesians 5, where Paul speaks of the filling of the Holy Spirit, you'll remember how he applies that. He doesn't say, 'When you're filled with the Spirit, your quiet times will all be wonderful; you'll have super-mystical experiences of Jesus.' He says, 'When you're filled with the Holy Spirit, sort out your marriage, sort out your family, and sort out your relationships at work.'

Now, is that how you judge whether you're filled with the Holy Spirit today? 'What's my marriage like? Does my husband think I'm filled with the Spirit? Does my wife think I'm filled with the Spirit?' Let me ask you: if the filling of the Holy Spirit produces the character of Jesus Christ, when you come home from work, and you've just lost that contract on which your firm was relying, whom does you wife meet when you come through the door? Jesus? – or the worldly-wise businessman?

When your teenage children are pushing you just to see how far they can go, with whom do they have to deal? Jesus Christ? – or a mixed-up, middle-aged parent who's forgotten how to relate to his own kids?

For unless it's those areas – home, marriage and work – that are drenched in God the Holy Spirit, we have no right to say that we are living in His fullness. For that's how the apostle applies his teaching.

The question to ask is not how much of the Holy Spirit of God do I have, but how much of me does He have?

The power to proclaim

Look with me, will you, at the last two verses that I read.

The disciples had just had the death and resurrection of the Lord Jesus Christ. They had been told they were going to be the recipients of that which had been looked forward to ever since Joel. This is it! Look at what we can really achieve for Christ in the world now! You can feel them getting fired up for world mission, can't you?

Do you know what they ask him?

Look with me at verse 6: 'Lord, at this time, are you going to restore the kingdom to Israel?' – Are You going to kick the Romans out now?

They haven't got it at all, have they?

So what does Jesus say? Well, He tells them, first of all, that sort of thing is none of their business. And then He says, 'You shall receive power when the Holy Spirit has come upon you' – and the word is 'dynamite' – 'and you shall be my witnesses in Jerusalem and in all Judea and Samaria and to the end of the earth.'

If you want to say to me tonight, 'Bob, I experience the power of the Holy Spirit in my life,' then I want to ask you: How many people look to you, and want to ask what it is that makes you different, and come to faith in Jesus Christ because of your living testimony and your spoken, shared, gospel?

Peter is filled with the Spirit on three separate occasions before the end of Acts 4, and on each and every occasion it's the Word of God that takes another step forward. In chapter 2 he's filled with the Spirit, and three thousand people get converted from his sermon. In chapter 4, he's filled with the Spirit, and the Sanhedrin – the very court that condemned the Saviour to the cross – get to hear the good news of Jesus Christ. And at the end of chapter 4 he's filled with the Holy Spirit again, and the Church learns what real fellowship and sharing its possessions are all about.

The Holy Spirit does not come to send us on a super-spiritual ego-trip, He comes so that we may be witnesses of the Lord Jesus Christ.

If I were pouring water into a glass, what would happen if I didn't stop pouring? Everything would flow over, until the jug was empty. But imagine that glass standing at the base of Niagara! That is meant to be the Christian's life in the power of the Holy Spirit – so constantly filled with the power of God that no matter how much life takes out of him, no matter how much he has to expend in ministry, or she gets buffeted by the pressures of the world, it's the character of Jesus that flows over.

Now, is that your life and mine? – because maybe it isn't. If it's not, what is the Scriptural answer? Jesus said,

'If you being evil know how to give good gifts to your children, how much more will God give the Holy Spirit to those who – ask.'

Those of you who have children: When they come in from school, tired and thirsty, and say, 'Mum, Dad, can I have a drink and a biscuit?', you don't send them away with a flea in their ear, do you? And God won't send us away from this tent empty tonight – if we ask.

But you see, it's a daily asking, for every Christian, every day: 'Fill me with You, Lord, that others may find You through me.' The barometer of our fullness with God's Spirit is not what we feel, but the effect on the lives of those around us.

KESWICK 1988 TAPES

Here is a list of tape numbers for all the messages in this book. The numbers follow the sequence in the book.

The Bible Readings

Dr Donald English: 88/2, 88/3, 88/4, 88/5
Rev. Stuart Briscoe: 88/26, 88/27, 88/28, 88/29

The Addresses

Rev. Stuart Briscoe	88/1
Canon Keith Weston	88/15
Rev. David Jackman	88/16
Rev. Alistair Begg	88/18
Dr Donald English	88/19
Rev. Philip Hacking	88/21
Rev. Gordon Bridger	88/32
Mr Dick Dowsett	88/35
Rev. Robert Key	88/37

These tapes, together with a full list of Keswick tapes, can be obtained from:

The Keswick Convention Tape Library
13 Lismore Road
Eastbourne
East Sussex BN21 3BA.

KESWICK 1989

The annual Keswick Convention takes place each July at the heart of England's beautiful Lake District. The two separate weeks of the Convention offer an unparalleled opportunity for listening to gifted Bible exposition, experiencing Christian fellowship with believers from all over the world, and enjoying something of the unspoilt grandeur of God's creation.

Each of the two weeks has a series of four morning Bible readings, followed by other messages throughout the rest of the day. The programme in the second week is a little less intensive, and it is often referred to as 'Holiday Week'. There are also regular meetings throughout the fortnight for young people, and in the second week for children.

The dates for the 1989 Keswick Convention are 15–22 July and 22–29 July. The Bible Reading speakers are Rev. Philip Hacking and Rev. Chuck Smith. Other speakers during the fortnight are Messrs Victor Jack, Ian Knox and Peter Maiden and The Revs. Jim Graham, Paul Weston, John Samuel, Robert Amess, Donald Bridge, George Hoffman and Derek Bingham.

Further details may be obtained from:

The Keswick Convention Secretary
PO Box 292
Harrow
Middlesex
HA1 2NP